CONTENTS

Editorial 3

There's a bluebird in my heart that wants to get out 10

Footnotes After a Year of Struggle 19

Haunted by the Ghost of the Collective Subject 36

Justice? Just Us! 51

Memories of Movements: The Anarchist Train to the G8
in Scotland 60

Left Discontent and Right Refusal 78

Stick It to The Man 110

What if They Called a Pogrom and Nobody Came? 116

Three Notes on Thinking as an Organisation 142

Beneath the Tombstones, the Beach: An Interview With
John G., aka TheLitCritGuy 197

DELETE, Untitled

EDITORIAL

We decided as an organisation to put this publication together during our 2024 Plan C gathering in Bristol. The meeting itself was the first of its kind since the pre-pandemic period, and although Plan C has remained active in one way or another throughout the past years, this meeting was seen as something of a reboot moment for our organisation. It was here that we not only took the decision to work together on a physical publication, but also developed many of the ideas that would eventually be contained within it.

So why this publication and why now? 2025 marks a decade since the last print run of our short-lived BAMN magazine. Although Plan C has published many other articles and printed materials in the meantime, serving both as a platform for our own members to share political reflections, and as a venue for the ideas and reflections of others, it seems to us that what has been missing from all of this activity is a tangible collection of a wider range of perspectives and experiences from within the organisation itself. Our gathering in Bristol last year proved beyond all doubt that almost every one of us has some insight or reflection that they want or perhaps even need to share. But what crucially connects all of these interventions is the fact that they amount to more than a mere statement of political opinion. Instead, they are reflections from the point of view of struggle, be it in the context of everyday life, that of the organisation and political environment we exist within, our place within society, or even how we face up to and try to organise against transnational capital and the logic of war. The purpose of this publication is to try and capture a sample of the material struggles we are engaged in: political struggles we carry out as part of Plan C or other organisations we are connected to, but also social and personal struggles which our life as members of a revolutionary organisation helps us to make sense of without turning to dejection and despair. In these pages you will find accounts of workplace struggle, struggle against the arms industry and genocide, struggle within our own organisations and movements, struggle against a rising tide of racism, feminist struggle, struggle against closure and the impoverishment of political imagination... And at the same time there are many political projects we are engaged in, organisational and theoretical reflections, and personal perspectives which do not appear in these pages, a fact which for us most clearly indicates that this will be the first in what we hope to be a longer-running series.

The 10 or so years that have elapsed since our last printed publication also afford us an opportunity to see how the organisation has developed, how its composition and outlook has changed, how the political realities we relate to and try to intervene in have changed. What have we learned about ourselves as an organisation in that time, and what does it mean for the future? In some ways, the questions we ask ourselves now aren't altogether different to the ones we were asking then: questions about social reproduction, the politics of everyday life, the rise of the far-right and fascism, what it means to be a revolutionary organisation in the context of a complex world. All of these remain as relevant today as they did 10 years ago. On the other hand, one could argue that the stakes and defining characteristics of many of these problems have changed. Environmental politics have shifted from a peripheral position on the fringes of the left to one that is central to almost every revolutionary question. The shared experience of a global pandemic has opened up new and important questions around care, the democratisation of technology and science, and the very possibility of political organisation under conditions of catastrophe verging on social collapse. As we write, the Russia-Ukraine war has entered its third year and the creep of militarisation seems impossible to ignore. Far-right ideologues bray for the return of military service and increased arms budgets in every corner of Europe. Trump has begun his second term as US President and isolated himself within a conclave of

Peter Newell, *The Enchanted Typewriter*

Peter Newell, *Crash! Came the Rocket*

techno-fascists, one which includes the supposed richest man in the world. The grotesque clarions of reactionary nostalgia bleat their cries for war: war on women, war on the left, war on trans and queer people, war on the disabled, war on migrants, race war, trade war, land war, war against war wherever convenient, but war against those who cry for the war to end wherever not. Anything but class war, of course.

The ongoing genocide in Palestine has already left an indelible scar on our political consciousness that will not—and as a matter of historical responsibility ought not—be forgotten for the rest of our lives. We have borne witness to the stark contrast between images of an almost impossible brutality and the glib statements of world leaders, the press, and parts of civil society, even including some on the left, as they continue to lend moral and material support to Israel. We have been faced with the challenge of how to organise politically against such things when protest no longer seems to be enough, when the asymmetries of state and capitalist power seem too overwhelming to recoup the ambitions of revolutionary politics from the last century.

In the face of these conditions, it can seem even absurd to speak of the timeliness of a printed publication such as this one. Nonetheless, we see the need for such a thing to exist. Partly as a means of further developing our own political understanding and outlook by consolidating it for ourselves in a written format and by letting it stand to the test of public opinion. Partly in the hope that some of our own ideas and reflections can be of service to others who continue, in spite of everything, to struggle. No matter how hopeless our situation may at times seem, there remains the simple and constant truth that we must struggle, however we can, not simply

Émile Bourdelin, Compositor

as a matter of consoling ourselves that we are doing something, but with a genuine hope of winning. This publication, in the same vein, is not simply the outlet for a pent up and frustrated political scream. It is a call to action, to continue engaging in material struggle and to continue learning from the inevitable failures of that struggle so that we can learn to fail better. The words contained here are all meant, in one way or another, to provide something of practical import, to give a multitude of different readers from different backgrounds some material to reflect upon, to challenge, or to identify with.

With this goal in mind, we tried very consciously to put together a range of material, pitched at various levels of interest, some parts more theoretical, others concerned with the very practical matters of ongoing political projects and struggles. Some of the material is more literary and personal, whilst other contributions seek to engage not only through the written word, but also via images. This wide variety in both the style and substance of interventions reflects our organisation, which in the past number of years has increasingly sought to diversify the range of approaches and perspectives within itself, whilst at the same time maintaining something of its enduring identity which we all in one way or another continue to believe in as a meaningful political project. Some of these articles and essays will be more accessible, whilst others can be destabilising on entry but, we hope, worth the effort of engagement. Whilst we do not and have not ever as an organisation sought to shy away from complex questions and at times concepts that diverge from the language of the everyday, we have on the other hand spoken in ways that are always informed by the material and practical questions of political struggle and organisation. These are not in any sense esoteric interests, but rather the outcome of a very real set of reflections about what it means to think, act, and exist as a political militant in the 21st century. The number of issues and questions that urgently need discussion is far greater than what we were able to address in these pages. In the process of putting this publication together, we sought to give each author the freedom to express their thoughts in whatever level of detail and specificity they felt necessary. This is something we hope to continue in future editions, aiming for a depth of experience and insight instead of seeking breadth by ticking every box, but never quite allowing room to say something that has not yet been said on a subject.

The process of getting this publication to print was a lengthy one. Whilst we hope and expect that future editions will come to fruition with relative ease, now that we have managed to break the path with this first

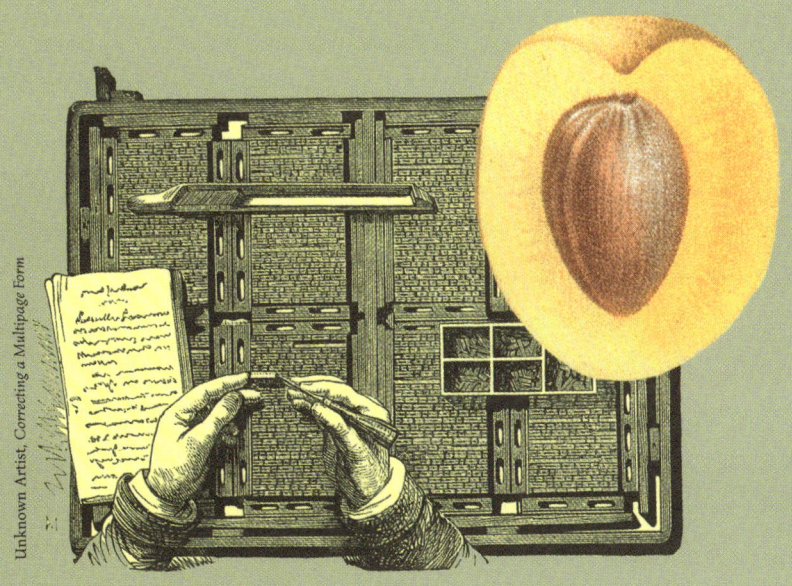

Unknown Artist, *Correcting a Multipage Form*

edition, it is worth reflecting a little here on the amount of logistical, organisational, and ultimately also reproductive labour that goes into such an undertaking. The price of the publication aims to cover some of the costs of printing, distribution, and various other overheads with a view to making this publication self-sustainable as a long-term project. The labour of organising all of these things, from the writing, to editing, to design, production, and all the other logistical and practical work involved on our part was done for free and from a sense of political necessity. We would like to pay our contributors, and especially those people in the process who have sacrificed enormous amounts of time and effort to bring this physical object into being, many of them living precariously, scraping by on low-paid jobs and social welfare, or others in full-time jobs who have sacrificed a great deal of their personal lives to continue this and other important forms of political work. None of these people expect to be paid, all of them have made such sacrifices unthinkingly and in the knowledge that the necessity of political work insists upon itself, with or without remuneration. As in all of our political work, we hope nevertheless that it can, in one way or another, eventually serve in some way that helps us to live, to reproduce ourselves through a form of production which we believe has value. Until then, being assured of the value that a publication such as this one might have for our comrades everywhere is enough to keep us going. ❧

Guillotines Editorial

Editors: **Enda O.**
Alessio L.
Olly B.
Ben H.
Sophia L.
Neil O.
Andrew X.

Proofreading: **Briar P.**
Neda G.
Enda O.

Design: **Flann D.**

Käthe Kollwitz, *The Carmagnole*

There's a bluebird in my heart that wants to get out

Morrigan

You can see it in their eyes, most of the kids I teach: wide, flat, a thousand yard stare that can only make it as far as the wall opposite. Yeah, they want to escape but they don't know what from or where to. And they've got no idea of how.

'If you've got a runner, always put them by the door and never get in the way of their exit.' Sure thing. Often they'll leave swearing loudly, not so much at me or about me, it's more like an explosion, and I don't want to get caught in the blast wave.

The thing about fight or flight is that it's messy, animalistic and incredibly noisy. It floods the senses and unhinges language. It will both try to stand its ground and make a break for it simultaneously. When we say that a student is 'heightened', we mean that they've become irrational, normal communication strategies are no longer viable, and they're a risk to themselves and others. It's not just the kids.

When I first started teaching here my colleague told me that it was one-third school, one-third psych unit and one-third prison. That's pretty accurate. The level of need is very high. Based in a working class area of a relatively affluent town, these kids come from families that are essentially destitute. The level of violence in the community involves everything from murder to your bog standard neglect. Addiction, abuse and the struggle to survive are the norm. It's traumatising.

About 10 years ago, when my own kid was in hospital, I started reading *At the Mind's Limits* by Jean Améry. Admittedly, not a great choice to dig into a Holocaust survivor's analysis of pure fear while sitting in an overcrowded NHS A&E department, however, it was what I had in my bag. Améry makes the point that those who had manual skills, who'd learned how to take something apart and put it back together again, who thought in mechanical ways, did much better in the camps. The intellectuals, on the other hand, who kept looking for reasons, who tried to apply rationality to the situation, were tortured by their inability to find any answers. They drove themselves mad. They gave up much quicker than the labourers and carpenters and tailors.

Primo Levi, in *If This is a Man*, tells us that at Auschwitz he once grabbed an icicle because he was thirsty but a guard snatched it out of his hand. He asked the guard 'Why?' and the guard replied 'Hier ist kein Warum' ('here there is no why'). Claude Lanzmann (the director of *Shoah* (1985)) uses this as his guiding principle when making what some consider a seminal documentary (and others consider a masterpiece of Zionist propaganda). Eight hours long! I've watched it three times. It's virtually impenetrable. But, Lanzmann's central argument is why there is no reason why, and why there cannot ever be a reason why.

Closure is what we're told we should look for after trauma. Apparently, it allows us to 'move on' and 'live our best lives'. We don't want to be 'trapped in the past'. That would be silly. No. Instead we need to understand, and once we can understand we can articulate, and if we can articulate, then we can change (Fugard after Freire). But what if the trauma is ongoing? How can you move past something that always keeps up with you? That sometimes overtakes you?

DELETE, Untitled

Yeah. You don't get to change a genocide. You don't get to change family members murdering each other. You don't get to change a lifetime of neglect from your addicted and abusive parents. These things feel fixed and burned into psyches, like those Hiroshima and Nagasaki shadows on pavements and buildings (Bataille after Hersey). Sure, you can recover from them, not saying you can't, but closure, flowing towards hope, that's another matter.

And Lanzmann says we shouldn't even try. At the point that we decide that's what we're doing, we're essentially looking for the easy way out. We want to shut it down to avoid any uncomfortable, irrational feelings. Because everything, now that we've emerged from the Dark Ages, can be reasoned away. There must be a logical explanation. Something that can redeem us.

It used to be God, that *volte-face* human/inhuman messianic principle. This life might be shit, but I will be saved. Saved from what? Saved by who? When? There's a million bodies in plague pits that say otherwise. And that's the deal. There's always the plague pits. Hope springs eternal from rotting bodies and twisted minds. 10% to the church and compliance with the Statute of Labourers (1351) and Peter will be laying out the red carpet right up to and through the pearly gates. Heaven is a place of reinvention so long as you're obedient: confess your sins, do your penance, 'Hail Mary, full of grace, the Lord is with thee; blessed art thou among women...'

I first learned what it meant to be a woman when I was six. My sister was pregnant. My (Catholic) mother explained how. I imagined it like lilies, sticky out bits and insidey bits. Despite the flowers and the lovely scent (to some), I still found it all a bit disgusting. My mother's insistence on using all the technical terms did nothing to assuage this.

Later I found out myself, but it was still confusing. I couldn't understand how my body wasn't generally mine. Three children later, I began to suspect that I had no rights over my actual person. I could be manhandled at will by (often male) gynaecologists, interrogated, subsumed as 'mere flesh' in their devotion to science. It wasn't so much that I was secondary, it was more like I didn't exist at all.

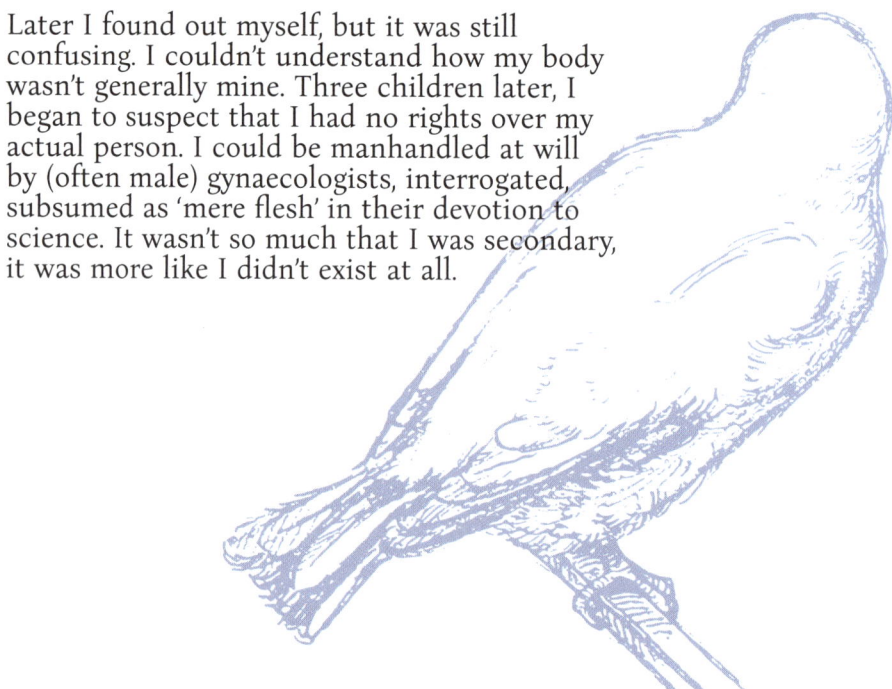

DELETE, Untitled

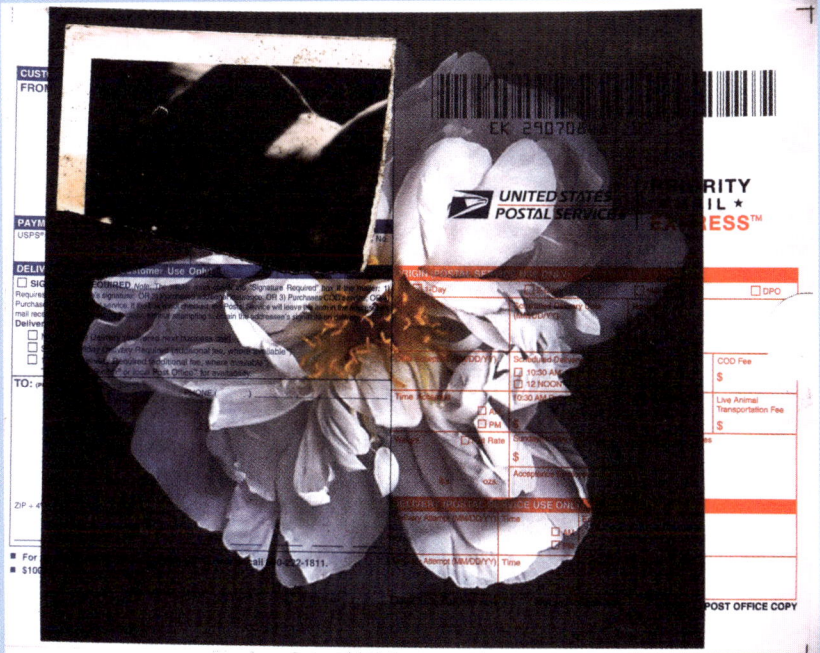

And the poorer I got, the worse it got. Husband in prison? All the hallmarks of a lowdown dirty bitch. Disabled baby? You must have done something wrong. Wanting to give birth in my own home? Delusional idiot. Are we sure that you're considering the best interests of your kids? We should probably come round and have a good look-see just to check.

In reproduction, my body became a warzone. It was a pitched battle for control. Women's fertility is always one of the sites of contestation, right from the abortion my mother couldn't get (and I'd hear about every time she was wrung-out and lost her temper with me) to the abortions we're still denied today. How can we be farmed like this? It's torturous. It's humiliating. And it's wrong. People with vaginas do not exist to provide nation states with soldiers or workers, in much the same way that land does not exist to provide towns and cities with food. Both are entities in their own right, free and independent.

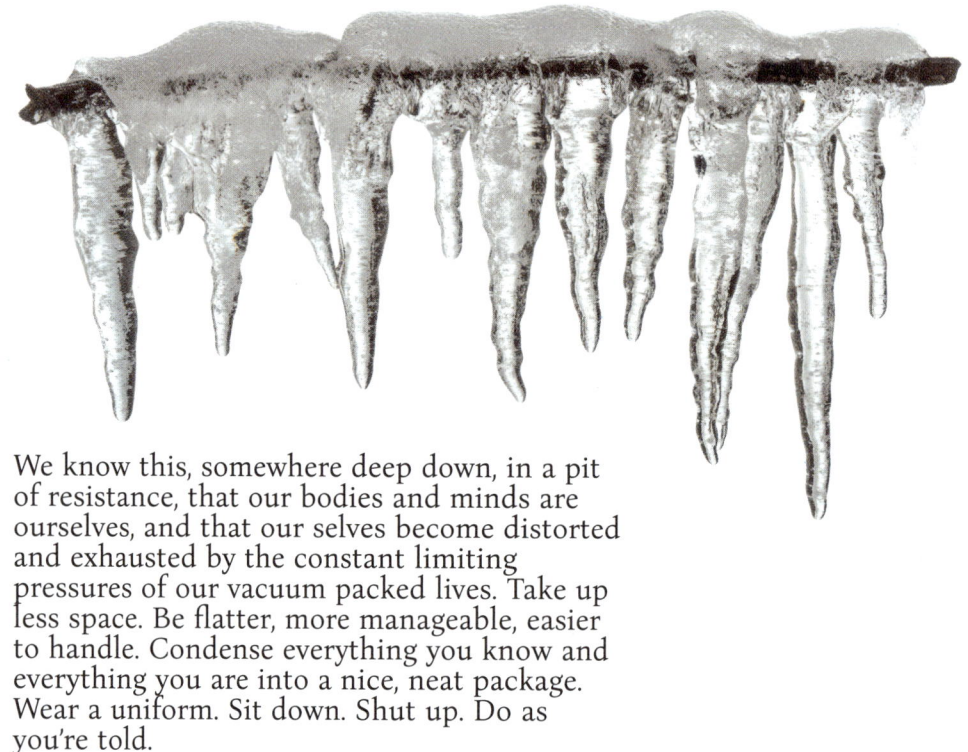

We know this, somewhere deep down, in a pit of resistance, that our bodies and minds are ourselves, and that our selves become distorted and exhausted by the constant limiting pressures of our vacuum packed lives. Take up less space. Be flatter, more manageable, easier to handle. Condense everything you know and everything you are into a nice, neat package. Wear a uniform. Sit down. Shut up. Do as you're told.

And so I look back at them, the messy and noisy kids in front of me, too scared to fly and too scared to fail. I don't have the key to the cage. The idea that education = liberation has become utterly and tragically recuperated, pretty much from the moment that Blair repeated the words on the gates of Auschwitz— because work doesn't make you free. Instead, it feels as if there's no escape, no redemption, and at some point or another we'll all become *Sonderkommando*, mired in filth and desperation and our own shame.

For now, I'll leave it to others to identify how we can solve the paradox of vertigo and/or the dangers inherent in remaining grounded when that's where the lightning strikes. In the meantime, my bluebird and me will take refuge in tiny corners, his wings and my heart fluttering, deep in the dead of night, waiting for the dawn to come and the storm to pass. One day, my friends. One day. ❧

DELETE, Untitled

Blanca D. & Charlie M.

FOOTNOTES AFTER A YEAR OF STRUGGLE

We were asked to draw out some learnings and reflections on the successes and challenges of the Palestine solidarity movement in the UK during the past year. The following text is an attempt to unpack the organising process of our experiences in Workers for Free Palestine (WFFP), an organisation developed after a series of direct actions responding to the genocide in Palestine, and that opened new possibilities for struggle in the UK.

We hope that these reflections are helpful for others in their own struggles. At the same time, another motivation in writing this is to document the activity we have been doing. This is an attempt to consolidate our learnings ahead of the next cycle of struggles, so that we are able to effectively organise further disruptive political actions. Through this conversation we extend an invitation for comrades to develop a collective analysis of the past year's organising in the UK Palestine solidarity movement. We also extend an invitation to people in struggle beyond the UK who have reached out to us regarding our experiences: people organising for better living conditions and for the transformation of the system.

Patrick Perkins on Unsplash

Towards an understanding of solidarity politics

Following the events of 7th October 2023, Israel unleashed over a year of terror on the people of Palestine – and subsequently the people of Lebanon and Syria. This was not the beginning but rather a continuation and expansion of Israel's colonial project of economic dominance and land capture. As its ongoing genocide of Palestinians continues, Israel has continued to develop itself as a model of the business-friendly state, strengthening its economic interests while making use of political and diplomatic cover, cultural legitimacy and aligned imperialist interests. We have also seen Israel develop new technologies of violence, while our own states become more effective in the repression of solidarity movements. Nevertheless, Palestinians remain undefeated in their struggle for liberation and self-determination, and the renewal of a new phase of transnational solidarity has strongly opposed this international coalition of colonial violence.

The acceleration of the struggle for Palestinian liberation demands a solidarity movement which continues to build and renew its forms of resistance.[1] We believe that in order for us to be able to respond to these circumstances it is essential to situate our responses by centring the idea of, and developing political practices rooted in, material and practical solidarity. After a year of multitudes taking to the streets, direct

---

1. There are many things to be said about the multiplicity of resistance, and the differences in roles in the struggles we take part in which don't fit in this text. In our perspective, the role of anti-colonial solidarity movements is to support the resistance flourishing in the territory, despite the contradictions that might arise from external political actors that are not operating under conditions of colonialism and war. Simply put, what resistance to colonialism looks like in a territory at war versus in a territory whose government materially and politically supports war and colonialism means different things, and ultimately our role is also to understand and respond to those conditions.

Nour Tayeh on Unsplash

actions, workers organising, hunger strikes, and student encampments, we are in a moment of renewal and experimentation in our activities and understandings of the possible forms of solidarity. Nevertheless, our efforts need to be directed. Material solidarity is a constant and ongoing question which guides us towards identifying choke points of the state's war machine and understanding how to strike it most effectively in the current context. When we started out organising as WFFP, material and practical solidarity meant moving beyond marches and trying to find a way for the mobilised masses of people to take strategic direct action in order to disrupt the production and transportation of arms from Britain (among other states) to Israel. In the beginning this looked like blockades at arms factories. However, at each step, we need to assess our strategy. Material solidarity doesn't just mean finding one disruptive tactic and running with it, it requires an ongoing process of material analysis combined with experimentation of practices.

So then, where did we find choke-points in the war machine? How did we decide to strike against it? How did we form strategy, tactics and demands?

Workers For a Free Palestine was born in October 2023 in response to the genocide and to calls from Palestinian workers and trade unions for action against the arms trade. It started by organising mass blockades of arms factories to disrupt the production and transportation of arms. According to our comrades inside, these one-day blockades temporarily shut down the arms factories and cost the arms companies millions of pounds, as well as starting conversations among arms workers in the factories. These blockades also shifted the national conversation around an arms embargo and led to shifts in the political positions of some of the trade unions and the mainstream Palestine solidarity movement.

Our decision to take these actions followed our material analysis of the key choke-points in this conjuncture. We shared an understanding that conducting war and colonial domination is not possible for a state without large quantities of weapons and munitions. During twentieth century wars, most states produced a significant portion of their own weapons and munitions, in which case supplies of key basic resources needed to produce those weapons and munitions – such as metals, fuel and raw ingredients for explosives – could be the most important choke-points. In the current moment, however, arms and munitions production is much more transnational and states are often highly reliant on supplies of parts from a wide range of different allied states. While the Israeli state does have some domestic arms production, it is largely reliant on arms produced abroad, specifically in the USA, Britain, Italy and Germany. Without the arms and munitions that are produced in these allied states, Israel would not be able to conduct its war and sustain its settler colonial project. For these reasons, we focused on the arms supply from Britain to Israel as the key choke point. There are other important choke points too – for example, the economic ties between businesses here and in Israel, which are targeted by the BDS movement. We felt that the arms supply was most important in this moment, and also most clearly implicated the role of our own state in support for Israel.

We articulated this as a demand for an 'arms embargo from below' with an understanding that we need to go beyond just making a demand and instead enforce it through direct action. We know that our states are deeply strategically invested in support for Israel and cannot be easily forced to enact an arms embargo, due to their imperialist interests in the region and also due to ideological and political ties. For this reason, the arms embargo from below focuses on disrupting the production, transportation, licensing and selling of arms in any way possible.

In WFFP, we focused on a strategy of blockades at arms factories while simultaneously organising with arms workers. Our decision in WFFP to specifically target arms production at factories originally began as a symbolic call to the wider movement in Britain to move towards an arms embargo demand. We wanted to get beyond the mere demand for a ceasefire, and towards a material way of pursuing this goal. Our strategy

Emad el Bayed on Unsplash

crystalised over the course of the first few actions. We hoped that we could ultimately scale up these factory blockades to have a greater disruptive impact (maybe national coordinated action, multiple days of blockades, etc). We chose the blockade as a tactic because we felt it was a form of action accessible to a much wider base of people than smaller direct actions. We hoped this would give us greater potential to scale up our movement into militant action that tests our collective power. Mass blockades involving hundreds of people also allowed us to take disruptive direct action while significantly reducing the risk of arrests (in numbers there is safety). There are also other organisations in our movement ecosystem who are pursuing different tactics. For instance, Palestine Action is focused on an attritional strategy of sabotage and disruption where small groups of people attempt to damage or block factories owned by a small, Israeli-owned arms manufacturer, Elbit Systems. Whilst we remain in solidarity with Palestine Action, the challenges of effectively organising against the arms industry demand a diversity of tactics rather than a singular approach at the movement level. For instance, some arms companies are too big to shut down through sabotage alone. Our aim was not to compete with other groups in the movement, but at the same time to pursue a different strategy centred on building long-term power through labour organising.

The group was heavily influenced by labour movement politics, and as such shared a belief that politically organised workers in arms production and transportation could shift the course of the current genocide. Ultimately, their power to halt the arms supply through action from the inside is much greater than ours from the outside, although pressure from the outside would be needed to move workers to action. This influenced our choice of tactics. Over

Levi Meir Clancy on Unsplash

the course of the first few actions we developed relationships with several arms workers and this became an increasingly central part of our approach. Our calculation was that by organising blockades that included large numbers of fellow workers, we would be more effective in winning over arms workers to our position than other tactical approaches, such as sabotage or groups that have tried to use an approach based upon shaming workers. This was in alignment with the work being done by Workers in Palestine[2] to coordinate with numerous arms and logistics workers in different countries to take action in their workplaces to block the supply of arms.

Many organisers will no doubt relate to the fact that some of our best strategic insights often occur on the journey home from an action. Another element of our strategy emerged on the coaches back from our first action, where those who had taken part started to discuss how they could take action in their own workplaces[3] to push their employers to cut ties with the arms industry and with Israel, opening up another angle of pressure on the arms companies and building a broader front of worker solidarity that extended beyond the focus on workers in the arms industry, while also supporting this front. We organised a series of large assemblies where people could come together to discuss how they could go about this work and made plans to do so. This developed into various initiatives in different sectors, such as higher education, healthcare, culture, and charities. Alongside other organisations, we also helped develop the Watermelon Index.

2. https://www.workersinpalestine.org

3. https://act.progressive.international/watermelon/

Jeremiah Amaya on Unsplash

Looking back, we continue to believe that focusing on the arms supply is vital. The movement in Palestine and in the diaspora continues to lead on this strategy, such as the Palestinian trade unions that issued the call for a focus on arms, and the Palestinian Youth Movement who have developed and escalated this strategy with a transnational campaign focused on the giant logistics company Maersk[4]. With time, the demand for an arms embargo has been popularised and the idea of enforcing an arms embargo has been picked up by many groups internationally that have pursued and continue to pursue direct action against the arms supply chain. However, our intention to escalate mass blockades in Britain led to a stalling point and it is important to reflect here a little on why. After the fourth factory blockade, our group had developed significant strategic differences surrounding the issue of targets. Throughout the course of our actions, there were many discussions about how strategic or effective it was to target only the factories (how do you measure the impact of a one-day closure on a multinational? How many parts of weapons systems actually being exported to Israel were effectively blocked? etc). We discussed shifting to targeting transportation and ports at various points. A key moment for the group occurred when we shifted our target from production sites to government buildings responsible for arms licensing, which led in turn to further differences around self-defence, our responses to police repression and how we take over the streets in an urban environment rather than at production sites in rural areas. There was also a limitation to the mobilisation strategies we could follow at the time: we based our strategy primarily upon mobilising through personal relationships and we reached limits in terms of the numbers of people that could be

4. https://www.maskoffmaersk.com

engaged in our actions. There were also tensions over the composition of the people we were mobilising for our actions and the need to broaden out who was involved. We weren't able to overcome these tensions which eventually led to a split in the organisation and a loss of capacity and confidence. As a result, we ended up with an exclusive focus on workers organising (within and outside the arms industry) and abandoned the strategy of blockades and direct action.

As a result of the factory blockades and frequent and ongoing leafleting visits to factories, WFFP and other groups we work with have made contact with workers in several arms factories in different areas of Britain. Not much can be said publicly about this, but some small groups of workers in these factories are beginning to organise themselves into groups and networks within their trade unions. These groups can be slow to build, but as with every labour organising initiative, a long-term effort is required if we are to have any chance of success. An account from one factory worker involved in this organising from the inside can be read in Long-Haul magazine[5]. Of course, prior to this point, there were moments of substantial confrontation with some workers during blockades, which led to discussions within our group about whether it was worth trying to organise with arms workers at all and/or whether the blockades were harmful to that goal. However, the progress made so far is a really significant step forward, providing hope for worker-led actions in the future.

---

5. https://longhaulmag.com/setting-an-agenda-campbell/

Regarding our efforts to encourage and support people to organise in their own workplaces: despite hundreds of people participating in our assemblies and a number of sectoral groups being formed, we are only aware of around 10 participants who went on to organise large numbers of their co-workers to take collective action pressuring their employers to cut ties with Israel/arms companies. This did include some impressive actions, such as a walkout in a university involving hundreds of staff and students. However, very few of these workplace initiatives were able to keep going to force material changes from their employers, although some are still organising together. Many other participants in the assemblies struggled to organise their co-workers even to the point of levelling a demand towards their employer. The assembly model was good for engaging large numbers of people and developing a baseline of shared politics together around a commitment to try to organise in our own workplaces, but it wasn't very effective for providing the ongoing support needed. We also didn't have enough people with sufficient experience of workplace organising involved in the project who could coach and guide people new to this through the sustained work required to make it successful.

Toa Heftibah on Unsplash

Building upon these reflections on what we have accomplished, we ask ourselves: how do we act most effectively in a new conjuncture? What kinds of organisational efforts are required?

It feels like we are not able to think about organising without considering the questions of urgency and time that shape the conditions of our organising. Over recent years we have increasingly experienced struggles under conditions of crisis and states of emergency. How do we[6] collectively respond to this urgency? People often talk about timing, building momentum, and how we can elevate our struggle in order to rise to the circumstances. Our organising is marked by urgency, which can provide conditions for new tactics to flourish, but also can dislocate and disable our movements. In these circumstances, we need to reflect on the state of movements of resistance in Britain and the structures we have in place to support us to respond with urgency in moments of crisis. It feels palpable that after four decades of neoliberal rule, the state of social movements and even the social fabric of Britain is, to put it lightly, weak if not disintegrating. There are not many collectives or structures that are able to run effectively, with sustained activity and economic independence— just a cluster of independent and autonomous organisations that are left over from the movements in the 2010s, with varying degrees of functionality. In the current circumstances, where cycles of struggle seem to intensify in shorter periods of time, and we are forced to organise under a constant sensation of crisis and urgency, this lack of structures, bases and political homes that people can turn to, and the lack of orientation towards revolutionary projects, makes it difficult for us to develop and test our capacity for collective power (not only through direct action but even for mobilisations, statements, coalition work, calls to action, etc). Collectively we are struggling to develop practices and organisations that strengthen our capacity to confront everyday violence.

---

6. This 'we' refers to a broad understanding of subjects in resistance, in a generous sense of who takes part in movements of resistance, that might refer to organised/active militants in independent, radical groups, but also others that are also involved in the multiple strategies pursued in social movements and who might be part of more formal/institutional structures (third sector, civil society, trade unions, etc).

Responding to urgency by building organisation

During the past year we have seen a myriad of campaigns, groups and collectives spring up, either geared towards institutional politics or electoral efforts, or towards building the capacity for direct action. It can be difficult to launch new projects like this from a standing start without preexisting organisation. There were a number of experiments; some were too ambitious to pull off and fell away. But the urgency of the crisis also allowed some projects to grow rapidly, as WFFP experienced. Nonetheless, a year and a half later, only a small number of these have continued. For us, it was essential that a new experimentation beyond tactics could develop out of this cycle. This could be done by gathering people around a common project and cultivating an organisation with the ability to define a path, deepen our understanding of organising for liberation, and develop new comradeship.

WFFP started with a group of seven activists from different backgrounds and struggles, organising initially through personal networks as a means to bring in numbers and building on trusted relationships. In 5 weeks we had organised two blockades and grown to 100 people in a chat. We were talking about organising coordinated national actions, about reaching thousands and about the responsibility, immediacy and urgency that we carry when taking a political direction. We decided to see who was in the room, what ideas, directions and experiments would arise from that energy. We asked comrades to bring proposals to a meeting. 60+ people showed up to the meeting and 15+ proposals got submitted. We were called upon by comrades to discuss what would come next. It was clear to Palestinian comrades that we needed to seize the moment and the energy and channel it beyond a response to current events. We needed to invest in a project committed to the long term. In that sense, we wanted to fill a gap in the Palestine solidarity movement in Britain, one that would allow for an autonomous organisation with a worker-oriented strategy and following direct action practices to respond to the immediate threats. We decided to shift the group into an organisation, which we believe was the correct approach in retrospect. If we are going to overcome the left's lack of strong organisations, then we have to start building them. But doing so brought its own challenges.

To build an organisation from scratch, in the midst of this politically urgent situation, without having built a base of trust and without an agreed-upon direction beyond a tactic, was difficult. A new organisation requires a number of different foundations, such as a common horizon, shared analysis, trust, collective principles, shared organisational culture, and defined decision-making structures. WFFP faced challenges developing these while trying to keep up with the urgency of the moment. It has taken a period of scaling back from some of the organisation's more intense activity, and months of work, to consolidate these things meaningfully.

We also faced challenges because of the lack of broader political infrastructure, which can mean that after the initial rush of energy, when people encounter obstacles or failures, they can quickly get burned out or disillusioned because there isn't a wider political movement to help hold things together. Nevertheless, we believe this was a good experiment to learn from for the next phase of the struggle. To build an organisation is a slow brewing goal, but it will allow us to develop collective practices, consensus and dissent that will clarify our politics in responding to the struggles to come. Against the instability, constant crisis, and criminalisation we need to continue to create structures that can foster collective possibilities.

Building an analysis of the interconnections between our struggles

In order to develop a consolidated and sustained movement, we also need to deepen our understanding of the struggle. In particular, we need to really break down how our struggles are interconnected, from the local to the international, in order to build a politics of joint struggle for liberation. This requires going beyond acting out of a moral sense of guilt or sympathy with people who are suffering. It also requires going beyond finding a 'common enemy' or shared targets across two struggles. Building a joint struggle means finding ways to articulate how our struggles are specific and where our struggles can be aligned. This sort of work is vital to enable us to sustain our solidarity work beyond the short term. For instance, we have seen how feminist struggle has developed in important ways by connecting questions of women's liberation to other material struggles surrounding debt and housing. It is not just a question of identifying these links in theory, but a matter of building links between existing struggles in practice. In WFFP, as we were building an anti-imperialist project in solidarity with the Palestinian people, we needed to try to understand and break down the ways in which imperialism articulates itself in our own territory. The British empire ruled over and laid the foundations for ethnic cleansing in Palestine and the British state continues to play an important role in supporting Israel and its colonial violence today, but imperialism also has shaped and continues to shape the living conditions of people in Britain. We need to work to understand how the imperialist project affected and shaped political, economic and social conditions in the UK. We need to understand that

David McLenachan on Unsplash

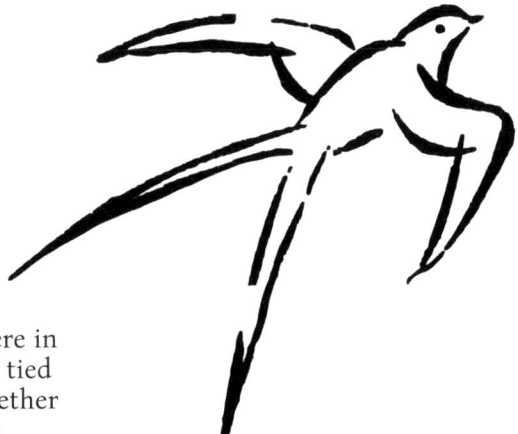

many of the problems we face here in our country today are intricately tied to the situation in Palestine—whether it's the lack of funding for public services due to expenditure on war, the dominance of global corporations who plunder from the Middle East as well as from our own communities, or the racist surveillance and policing practices that are brought back from Israel to London. However, there have been few attempts to develop this kind of analysis of how Palestinian liberation links into our everyday struggles in the UK and the local reality we confront in our own territory. Without a deep analysis of these links, we are likely to see our efforts weaken or even fall apart as the news cycle becomes oversaturated and moves onto the next crisis.

Over the past year, police repression has had a big impact on disarticulating organised people and groups. This, alongside the challenges, disagreements and tensions that arise organically in all forms of political organising, meant a rupture in our group, as well as many other parts of the Palestine solidarity movement. A palpable slowing down of the Palestine solidarity movement even before the recent 'ceasefire' shows that we have entered a new phase. Within these conditions we need more than ever to refer to the structures and organisations we have built. We also need to continue experimenting with our tactics and to figure out what a long term struggle outside the 'emergency' phase will look like. We need to continue identifying the choke-points of the war machine. After continued aggression and the escalation of violence from the Israeli state, most of us wonder what's next for the solidarity movement, where to head and how to continue strengthening our collective power. In a moment of exhaustion, it's difficult to imagine the new shapes in which the struggle can take form. But in any case, there's no other option.

Nour Tayeh on Unsplash

Conclusion

We cannot offer a complete reflection over what this last cycle has been, as organising continues to be developed and different campaigns, strategies and collectives adjust to current circumstances. With this article we wanted to draw out some of our experiences and some of the reflections that we thought were worth discussing, and to put them out there for our comrades to do the same. We believe in centering material solidarity, in joint struggle, in building structure, and in deepening our politics in order to be able to sustain our organising. We hope what we have shared will be useful for comrades near and far.

There are still many questions and learnings we are working through individually and in our collectives. In WFFP itself, comrades are currently working out strategy for the organisation going forward over the next phase. Nevertheless, we thought it might be useful to end with some questions to continue this conversation between comrades and fellow organisations:

☞ How do we address the disintegration of larger base movements and the weaknesses of the revolutionary left in Britain?

☞ How does our experience compare to your experience of WFFP and/or the wider Palestine solidarity movement?

☞ Where do the experiences of the past year lead us in terms of experimenting with new forms of political action moving forward?

☞ What are the next steps for solidarity movements, where should we go from here?

☞ How can we overcome some of the impasses and challenges we identified above?

☞ How can we build and incorporate workers movement strategies into solidarity work? 🌺

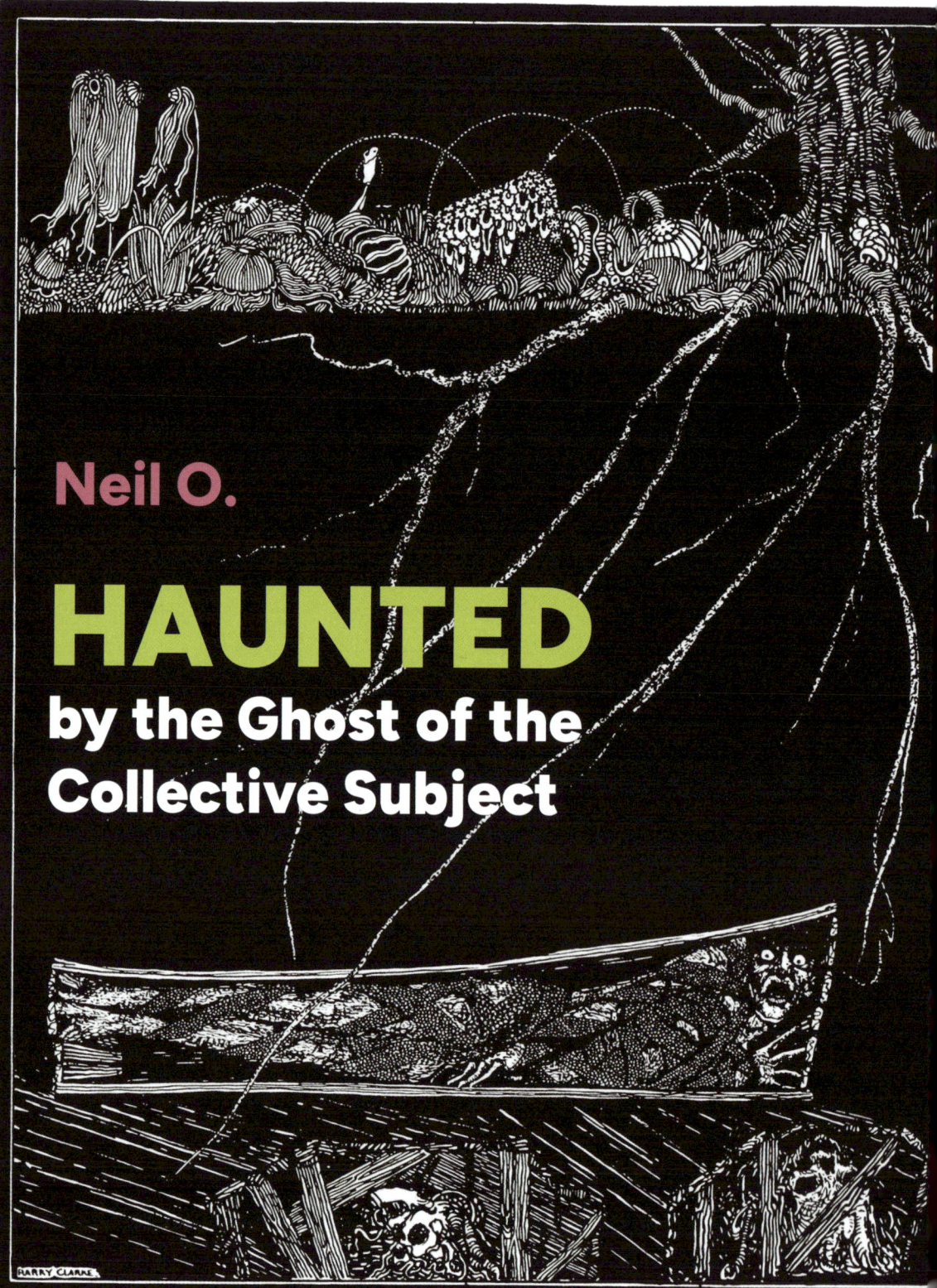

Neil O.

HAUNTED
by the Ghost of the Collective Subject

How the absence of social infrastructure prevents popular left ideas from gaining mass support. Why building trust, agency and mutual aid are the keys to building class confidence and power.

At the end of 2019 the journalist Sam Kriss wrote on his blog[1] about the failure of Jeremy Corbyn's attempt to win an election based on progressive policies:

'Labour was speaking to the ghost of a collective subject. People liked these policies, but the social infrastructure for their realisation simply wasn't there. For the strategy to have been effective, the collective subject would have had to already have been constituted. But the work of constituting it has not been done.'

Typically, what are considered left ideas (like nationalising public utilities) are supported by the great majority of the population. For example, three quarters of people support nationalising energy, trains and the post office, while 82% support nationalising the water industry. Support for measures to fight pay inequality runs at similar levels. Almost everyone likes the idea of more free time, higher pay, and affordable housing. But the organised left is tiny and irrelevant to these conversations. So the question is, why don't people believe that these very popular ideas can even be demanded, let alone achieved?

The single biggest and most important factor holding back progress lies in the splintered and atomised communities that we live in, and the lack of social infrastructure that would allow people to see themselves as part of a wider collective project. Because of this, our most pressing and urgent task is to rebuild (reconstitute) that collective subject – enabling us to feel our collective power and opening up the possibilities of what we can achieve together.

Capitalism Rules Everything Around Me

We live in a capitalist world, which has come to be dominated over the past 50 years by the ideas of neoliberalism: competition has been driven into almost every aspect of our existence. Everything in our lives has been financialised, monetised, Uberised. We have been taught to see each other as competitors.

---

1. https://samkriss.com/2019/12/19/the-case-for-giving-up/

C.R.E.A.M.

'Neoliberalism has been extremely effective at decomposing society. One of its primary aims has been to change our common sense view of the world and remove the preconditions for collective action ... Markets are imposed on ever-wider areas of life, and participation in those markets trains people in a neoliberal world-view. To explain this further: when you participate in a competitive market you are forced to act as a utility-maximising individual - you have to act in ruthless and heartless competition with others over scarce resources. The more we do this, the more we come to adopt this outlook as natural ... the possibilities that appear open to us are conditioned by these experiences.'

The Free Association 'Re:generation'

On top of this process, for the past 15 years austerity economics have ravaged public and community services. Housing costs and low pay are exhausting us. The NHS is on its knees. Even the roads are falling apart. Those 'scarce resources' have become even harder to reach. You would have expected the country to be in a rebellious mood, but there's nothing much happening. Neoliberalism has us turning on each other instead.

Despite all of this, many people are desperate for change, but just don't believe it will come. We are squashed by the weight of inertia and fear. We don't see a way for change to happen, and part of the reason for that is everyone else. We don't believe that we can rely on other people not to fuck it up. We think other people are selfish (but not me!), other people are stupid (but not me!). Other people won't stand with us if we take the risk of challenging authority (but I would!). In theory there is broad support for all kinds of progressive social and environmental policies, but we are deeply sceptical about other people. Because other people take advantage, other people can't be trusted. So where we have ended up now is that we aren't just competing with each other, but are actively suspicious and distrustful of 'everyone else'. The antagonism is (internal) within our class and not (external) between the classes. We have turned it on ourselves. Anyone who has worked in the public-facing side of the service industry (about 80% of the jobs in the UK) will have the experience of being shouted at, abused and treated as an enemy by other people (who probably experience the same shit in their own jobs), just for being in the way—either in person or at the end of the phone. Ironically, this shared experience is not bringing us together as a collective subject to challenge the status quo, it is driving us further away from each other.

DELETE, Untitled

Alien Nation

Living and working together could build a positive collective interaction, but instead capitalism imposes competition and hierarchy. Because our lives are defined only by our relation to capital and not in unmediated relationships between us, we are estranged from each other. Widespread loneliness and isolation pervade society at a time where people are more interconnected than at any previous point in human history, and where communication technology is more readily available than ever before. Social media could have led to an enormous expansion of human cooperation but has instead been driven by capitalist social relations to create an explosion of loneliness. The 'social networking service for neighbourhoods' Nextdoor (an app that allows people to talk to their neighbours without leaving home) is a perfect example of where this estrangement has taken us—into a quagmire of misanthropy, suspicion and racism.

Théophile-Alexandre Steinlen, from *Le Chambourd Socialiste*

Issues that affect millions of people have been individualised and hidden (made invisible). The moment of struggle has now become individual (made personal). You're on your own at a counter, in a cubicle, in your van, at a screen, in your home. Right at that moment we need to feel that other people share that situation with us (it's not just you) and support us. That you're part of something and you're not alone. Right at that moment we need to know that we can trust in other people. To not just feel that we're part of something but to really be part of something.

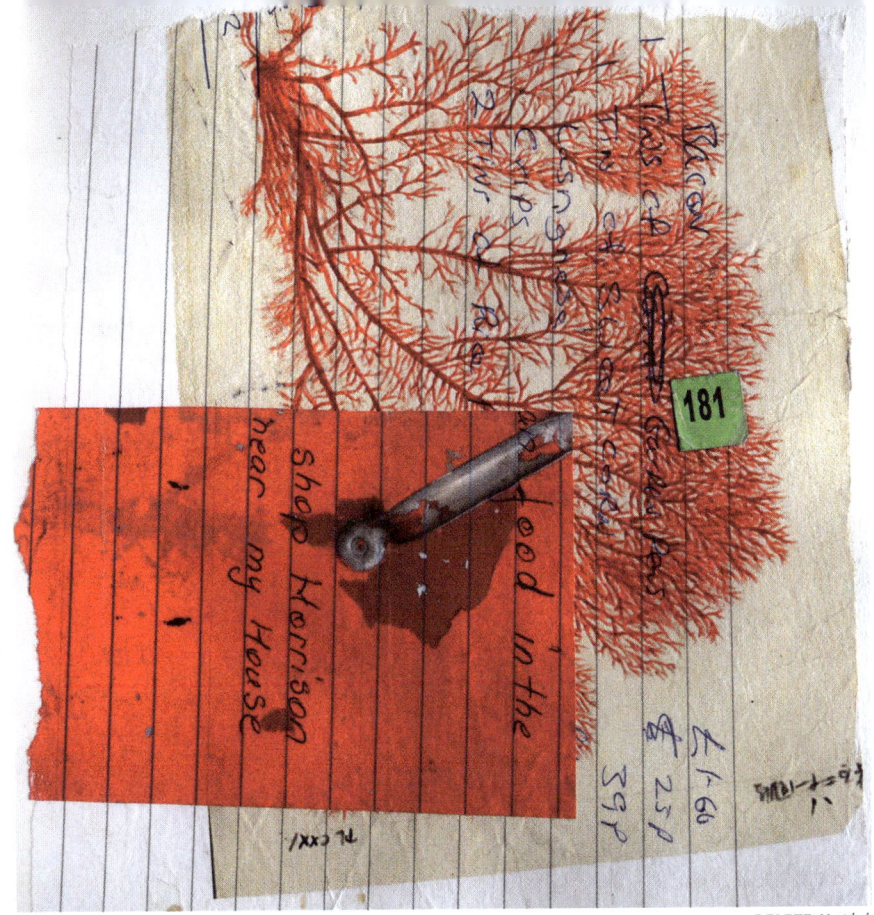

DELETE, Untitled.

Look What You Could Have Won

Older activists will remember how there used to be all kinds of social structures and shared experience/support. Until relatively recently it was possible to talk about a collective subject (as in a group of people with shared/common interests). There were collective projects everywhere, it was part of our working class culture. Community centres, youth clubs, pensioners' groups, social clubs, unions, union halls, working men's clubs. We had shared workplaces or shared experiences. These things have virtually (LOL) disappeared, a process that has snowballed since the start of the 21st Century. The majority of local organisations have become an almost distant memory, such that even just acting together (collectively) is a radical act by itself. Community networks that would once have spread news of (the impact of) cuts or fightback or support have disappeared (fragmented). Union membership is low and many unions have become less the tools of class power and more of a way to sell you insurance. Neoliberalism has helped to shatter our communities, through what sociologist Pierre Bourdieu identifies as 'a programme of methodical destruction of collectives'.

DELETE, Untitled

How It Starts

'The politics of separation can only be challenged by the politics of solidarity.'

Bini Adamczak

All this is to say that we are in a very difficult situation. We have demands, which resonate with many people. But none of our demands are currently seen as 'realistic' because the means of achieving them are not visible (either not present or don't even exist). Without some form of visible, practical social infrastructure it's hard to see how we will be able to persuade enough people to support our demands (however much they sympathise with our ideas), let alone put themselves on the line to achieve them. There's a tendency for us to focus a lot of time and effort on honing our message or strategy into the best version that we can possibly achieve, but in this context there's a real danger that no matter how good our ideas are, or how widely and effectively they can be circulated, they cannot succeed.

We can only win collectively, that's a fundamental lesson of struggle. If we agree that this is true, then the only question is: how can we build these networks of care and support that will allow us to recognise each other as friends, allies and comrades? There are lots of ways that we could build this infrastructure, but why not start with what's already there and work towards making that into something more powerful and more effective? Something that's going in a more useful direction.

We can start by working with the remnants of people and groups who are still active, the fragile ecosystem that makes up what's left of our existing social infrastructure. Across towns and cities some people are involved in one or more single issue groups, support groups or union branches. They do this because they care particularly about that issue—and these groups are vital and their work is often very important. Many of these groups have shared interests but don't work together, except for one-off events. They often don't communicate, except that some individuals are active across multiple groups.

'Look at things as they are, face your prospects with brutal honesty.'

Stuart Hall

To be brutally honest, what these groups are doing now won't deliver the change we all want. We're not telling anyone that we know better and we're not telling anyone that they have it wrong—or saying anything that they don't already know. People who run food banks know they're not going to change the world, they're responding to a desperate situation the only way we currently can in this society. The anti-Poll Tax campaign of the 1990s built a huge network of opposition across the country which led to riots, the end of the Poll Tax and eventually the downfall of Margaret Thatcher. Both her and the Tax were just replaced with more politically acceptable options. The protests against the invasion of Iraq in 2003 brought millions of people out on the streets of London (as part of the largest protest in human history) to be simply ignored and for the huge movement that created it to fizzle out shortly afterwards. The Palestinian Solidarity movements in opposition to the genocide in Gaza have created new networks and possibilities for action, and in some areas changed the political landscape. In response the government has brought in new laws and the police have gained more powers. All these movements express the strength of collective action, all of them are important parts of our history.

The change we need is bigger than anything that any of us is doing individually or even in our organisations. We can all keep on plugging away with what we're doing forever and we will make some things better (it's better to do this than to do nothing, of course) and we will help some people, save some people. But ultimately, we will get to the end of our lives and the basic problems we've been struggling against will all still be there. If we want to make real change, make everything change (help everyone, save everyone) then we can't keep on doing it like this. We need big, structural, fundamental change. That means getting everyone involved.

Harry Clarke, *Silence*

How It Goes

How this process of recomposition could start is by going to each of your local groups and pitching the idea of a solidarity network, to weave and connect different initiatives together. For example, Group A works with refugees; Group B is a food co-op, guerilla gardening group or allotment committee; Group C is housing support or a renters union. By match-making these groups together Group B could provide food to Group A's refugees. The refugees from Group A could help with the gardening project or with food distribution. Group C could facilitate access to gardens for Group B, get food to tenants who need it or get Group B to train them how to garden. Connecting Group A and C together could enable a buddying or hosting scheme. With a growing network of contacts, we can expand these match-making possibilities, intertwining people who need something with people who have it. Whether that is a physical thing (food, clothes, shelter), know-how, support or just numbers of people. And we build and spread the idea, and build and grow, reaching places we couldn't before. And build and grow until the collective subject is no longer a ghost.

The glue that binds all these groups together is mutual aid. Mutual aid is a voluntary giving or lending of resources, labour or goods to others in a shared community with the expectation that the entire community will in turn benefit. We currently live in a society where everything has a price, everything costs something or must be paid for (everything has become a commodity). We're trying to break that relationship and we can't do it by demanding something in return.

Mutual aid challenges the current system by specifically not demanding something from people, because it is about creating a community that is not based on commodity exchange. Refusing to participate in exchange has the subversive potential to undermine the whole relation. Because solidarity isn't a commodity. We're building around a new relation, but it's not an exchange relation. It's a solidarity relation. Exchange is the practice of releasing property on condition of receiving an equivalent in return. Mutual aid is not a form of exchange. It's not a swap shop or a time bank. Mutual aid is not charity, nor is it some kind of bartering system.

Mutual aid is freely given help to others in our community. The idea is that as individuals in the community help each other the entire community benefits and that in turn supports the individual's own goals. It's about building something based on cooperation and solidarity. It's in all of our interests to build this infrastructure—whether or not it addresses the things or political interests that we are most directly concerned about or not—because on the back of it we can build a broad consensus of what is possible and how we can achieve it. We show each other that we understand that we have similar problems that we have to deal with. We build trust. This is transformational activity which affects everything else we are struggling for across the board. And without that we are just pissing in the wind. We all have lots of perfectly legitimate demands but they are totally unobtainable in the current situation.

Mutual aid can help us to identify and learn and practice the skills that we will need to change the world. In these networks we have the potential to grow, through the process of figuring out how to work with each other, how to get through obstacles, how to deal with complexity, and how to build collective communication. We will learn about each other, how to identify our strengths and weaknesses, how to share information, experience and knowledge. How to debate and discuss, creating consensus by ensuring that people can express themselves freely and safely and challenge others freely and safely. By working together in this way, we can learn to identify our self-interest with that of others, to establish mutual support for each other and understand our mutual needs. We may develop problem-solving, collective organising and decision-making skills. We can build the power to take risks, to practice autonomy, and most of all to feel the strength in our numbers.

Solidarity is a Process

As things stand, people are expected to make change without meaningful agency, so it's no wonder that they are constantly disappointed and resentful of those who ask for their support. We need to build ways to create agency, build the power to make change. We need to act in ways that have an effect. This will in turn create trust and rebuild connections that have been lost—or build new ones that were never made previously. Networks of possibility and power.

'The modern left is constantly trying to repeat strategies that came at the END of many decades of slow prefigurative construction throughout the 1800s and they keep being confused when they aren't able to conjure the same power on the fly.'

Daniel Baryon

DELETE, *Untitled*

We need to find a way to show that it IS possible to change everything. And to do this in a realistic, practical, achievable way. This means showing it works. This means building the infrastructure that will allow people to see what can actually be done. To get people to believe in the possibility of change, we need to show that it's real. We need to break the idea that 'you're OK, it's just everybody else'. We have to build the social infrastructure that can demonstrably achieve change, show people that they can trust each other, rely on each other, and work together. There is no-one else that can deliver the hope for a new future, just us, ourselves. If you want to wait around for someone else to do the work, you will wait forever.

Solidarity networks have existed before. What is different about this proposal is that we explicitly talk about how none of these groups will succeed on their own and that by acting together, we can make a bigger challenge. We have to go out and convince these groups that it is essential that we work together to build something greater than the sum of its parts. Many of the people organising these groups are not even on the left, they are from all kinds of positions and none. But all these people are what Bernadette McAliskey calls the 'could-be left'.

Harry Clarke, *The Dagger Dropped*

Let's be very clear. This is not party building. This is not recruiting, not manipulating, not using others for our own purposes. These networks are not going to deliver a communist future by themselves. But they are a prerequisite for any movement for change.

'Because participants are united around demands, they do not need to share the same values. For us to be political allies, I don't need to be converted to your religion and you don't need to meet my parents. Our reasons may be different but we still agree on the demand. Political alliances are successful despite values not because of them; they thrive when people stop trying to agree on fundamental philosophies so as to get something specific done.'

Alan Finlayson

Olly B.

JUSTICE? JUST US!

For over a decade, Plan C has included a Care and Justice group (C&J). It takes much from transformative justice ideas.

Care is central to human existence—despite what we are sometimes encouraged to believe, we are pretty stuck if we don't give and receive care for each other when we are children, when we are adults, when we are ill, when we are old and when we are hurt. It is a capitalist myth that anyone can survive, let alone live, without receiving or giving care. It is that essential.

Justice is equally vital—a means to recognise, address and resolve harm done by one or more people to others. There are far better approaches to hurt and harm (injustice) than carceral (prison and punishment-based) approaches, which are typically painful, demeaning and humiliating, punishing the 'offender' rather than making sure 'the offence' is understood as negative and aiming to reach agreements about how not to repeat it.

We have learned through Care and Justice's activity that there are ways to facilitate constructive resolution and to hold our members and others to account when necessary. We are acutely aware that when organisations hold 'internal investigations' this can lead to abuses, so our processes are informed by this very problem. We are committed to seeking resolutions which are constructive and transformative, rather than punitive, and we aim to treat all members and non-members involved in an equal manner. Nobody is considered to be above reproach. We value transformative justice methods.

What is transformative justice? Sounds like an action movie

Transformative justice means, we think, developing the capacity for justice independently of the State. This idea has been developed by Black and queer feminists in America over the last fifty years or so, arising from oppressed communities – for them the state was never a solution to the violence in their lives. It connects with the history of working-class solidarity, in rejecting any positive role for the state. Calling the cops never helps and generally makes things a million times worse. Communities of resistance to the cops and the state have to develop other ways to care for themselves, make themselves safe and find justice.

Where hurt is caused by one or more people to others, we believe that a fair process cannot be based on a starting assumption that those being accused are inherently toxic and 'beyond redemption'.

We believe that we could all gain much when we hold our friends, family members, neighbours, workmates, comrades etc. accountable for hurtful and harmful behaviours, in ways that are dramatically different to the legal and penal system, and which should be focused on specific behaviours rather than character generalisations.

Where harmful acts or patterns of behaviour have taken place, we think it's best to strive for a mutually agreeable resolution which enables individuals to feel safe and allows those who have acted badly to work on and resolve harmful behaviours. In essence, our aspiration is the development of a model of justice centred on care, compassion and understanding. This is how we understand the term 'transformative justice'.

Yeah, but what about the hurt?

We don't shy away from the anger and pain that harmful behaviours generate but we believe that this must be balanced with compassion, so that achieving meaningful justice actually makes a positive difference, achieved by us. In trying to balance these two elements—anger and compassion—we believe that transformative justice involves approaches which:

- Do not rely on the state (e.g. police, prisons, the criminal legal system)
- Reduce or eliminate harm and do not reinforce or perpetuate violence
- Rely on honesty
- Ensure accountability
- Produce resilience
- Create a safer environment where further harm is far less likely to occur

This is not to say that people who cause hurt should receive a big group hug and that's it. Being accountable for the injustices we have created can be painful and means accepting that your actions have caused pain to others. It also means a commitment to address and alter your behaviours and your thinking. Your accountability is ongoing and you aren't absolved simply by saying sorry.

If we're serious about growing transformative justice as a far better solution to harm and abuse, we have to be driven by solidarity and comradeship and not by prejudgements, assumptions and scepticism. Too often, accountability processes fail in practice, causing further trauma to the survivor of harm, unable to count on the cooperation of the 'offender'. But until we have built robust processes with mutual consent, we will continue to find that 'justice' is either delivered by the carceral state or 'administered' through rumours, moralising outrage, and unaccountable backroom decisions. Sadly the left is no stranger to the latter approach.

But surely the left usually manages well?

Absolutely not! There are often serious problems of sexual and other forms of abuse, intimidation and harassment within the left, and there are inadequate arrangements and support structures to provide an alternative to carceral justice or unaccountable decisions. We shouldn't be surprised that left organisations can reflect the violence and harm present in capitalist society. No-one can escape the influence of the injustices we are fighting against, but we can be aware of them and deal with their effects.

Rather than just seeing major issues like sexual assault, abuse and bullying as problems of individual conduct, we should recognise that they have a role of discipline and control under a heteropatriarchal system. This means that exposing and dismantling these tendencies in left organisations is very important. If we don't, we are failing, we are weakened and ultimately, we all suffer, while the state stands by, smiling.

We can't rely on punitive and exclusionary processes served on individuals while leaving their behaviours unchanged. This can be disastrous, mirroring the effects of the state's prisons. For example, sex abusers have been excluded or cancelled, only to emerge in another geography and repeat the abuse elsewhere. When this and similar things happen, in Mark Fisher's words, such an exclusionary (cancelling) tendency is 'doing capital's work for it'.

Razorsmile

We need transformative justice models to put this right, where it is often friends and close comrades who are best placed to help an abuser change their behaviour and make amends. They should be supported to do this, rather than being negatively labelled as 'friends of the abuser', complicit in their bad behaviour.

Many of us come into the left as young people. Meanwhile, despite our intentions, authority in left groups is usually held by established members of the group, often older, more assertive people, usually cisgender men. These power dynamics are very similar to those of the patriarchal society we reject.

Often political ties can be strengthened or damaged by the ups and downs of sexual relationships and close comradeship. Even outside such relationships, we have strong emotional ties to our comrades. At the best of times, comradeship is something indistinguishable from love. At the worst, these bonds can lead to harm, causing us to lose clear sight of group and individual discipline and accountability, in favour of the people we love and/or have sex with. It's therefore quite usual for left organisations to be environments of high emotional tension, where personal disagreements can lead to lasting hostilities between individuals and groups. At times of tension and anger it can be very helpful to remember that, essentially, we're on the same side, in the same struggles, fighting the same oppression, but maybe with different or nuanced points of view. We are also all human and humans tend to fuck-up from time to time.

Some steps forward

In our 2021 article, itself a reflection on our attempt at a transformative justice process triggered by allegations made by one or more members of an anti-fascist assembly in London, we discussed the dangers of some anti-fascist formats, which can transfer the emotions of confrontation and violence encountered in struggling against fascists and far-right activists, to relationships within our own groups, which in turn can breed in-group masculine aggression and abuse. We suggested that if anti-fascism isn't allied with feminism, control of masculine aggression may be far too weak.

To paraphrase the late David Graeber, if we act as if we are already free, we can begin to know what being free looks like. At the heart of such freedom is dealing with the ways we screw up as well as the ways we succeed. Opposing machoism, a tendency that some left activists display, means everyone taking a fair share of the social labour which a liberated society requires—caring for each other has to be central to this, not an afterthought after people have been hurt or abused.

When there are calls of abuse, they need to be investigated but the processes we use to do this have to be well-defined so that there is clarity and no chance of discrediting or denying harm that has been done. This is hard, particularly in tight-knit groups, but it can be achieved, enabling groups to thrive rather than to destroy themselves in bitter arguments or repeating the behaviours we have when fighting oppression.

NOTHING ABOUT US WITHOUT

We have seen the damage caused when groups close ranks to protect someone seen as a 'longstanding good comrade' who also happens to be an abuser. A strong group mindset is of course a strong basis for unity and organisational power, but we need to protect ourselves from doing the wrong things for the right reasons.

Just as we are socialised into violence, we are also socialised into a solution to violence: shunning and exclusion. In short, punishment. The effect is half carceral (hiding the offender by cancelling them) and half vengeful (make the offender feel the pain they've caused). Punishment has been a poor cure for violence in capitalist society—people in and leaving prison aren't usually peaceful and calm.

There's no reason to expect left movements or a liberated society to be miraculously free from interpersonal harm, so if we accept that harm is going to happen, the focus has to be on healing through justice that is transformative. This means making space for learning, growth, and even reconciliation.

OK, sounds good. What about putting words into action?

We're mindful that what might work for Plan C, through its Care and Justice group, may well not work for other groups and other day-to-day settings. But we think that it's no longer enough for us all to just do things our own way, in our own little space.

We need to collectively develop our communities' and the left's knowledge and capacity to deal with violence and abuse. We think we need to find a way to build trust in each other and between organisations and collectives. Perhaps this means developing some sort of 'conflict council' between organisations, where different groups can talk to each other about problems. Perhaps it means developing a wider, deeper understanding of transformative justice practices within the left. It certainly means changing the way we communicate with each other—at the heart of justice is a kind of confidence in each other, one that is not given but that we have to create in our practice.

We are keen to discuss with others how we build an infrastructure of transformative justice within the wider left. As we know, the state uses any means it likes, including sowing distrust amongst us, so we need to be able to deal with this. It's not just that we want to be able to care for each other, we also want to ensure that the toxicity of capitalism is not allowed to fester within the left.

Our capacity to build a future free of oppression depends on our ability to survive and heal the violence inflicted on us. Only in this way can we become free. We hope that Plan C can make a positive contribution to build our collective capacity to hold one another and ourselves to account, based on principles of and a commitment to effective transformative justice processes.

Notes:

As we were thinking about transformative justice and what it was for this article, we listened to Mimi Kim and Shira Hassan from America talk about *'The modern roots of transformative justice'* over on YouTube here from the Barnard Centre for Research on Women:

https://www.youtube.com/watch?v=ZqMxNiKQLHc.

We also watched the workshop on *'Sexual Violence and Transformative Justice in Abolitionist Times'*, with Mimi Kim, Shira Hussan, Ejeris Dixon and Leah Lakshmi Piepzna-Samarasinha. You can find that here:

https://youtu.be/VgRGWahX7wk (TRIGGER WARNING discussion of sexual violence).

We read Adrienne Maree Brown's book *'We Will Not Cancel Us, and other dreams of transformative justice'*; and have taken inspiration from the work of Cindy Milstein.

There are many voices involved in this discussion of transformative justice, but these can be some good starting points if you're unfamiliar with the concept or unsure what people mean when they use it. 🌺

Razorsmile

All artwork by Jody B.

MEMORIES OF MOVEMENTS: THE ANARCHIST TRAIN TO THE G8 IN SCOTLAND

Alessio L. and Jody B.

G8 summits have been places where international trade laws, regulations, and so-called 'structural adjustments' have embedded virulent models of development into international flows of capital.

These policies proposed and agreed at the summits create the structure of global and local economic systems, with the associated accelerating ecological disasters and the hollowing out of the 'public' state through never-ending austerity. They have subsequently created the rules that govern our everyday lives.

The emergence of so-called polycrises is a feature, not a bug, of contemporary capitalism. Anti-capitalists described these emergent crises at the time. Crises have been designed into global systems through a series of dramatic neoliberal reforms orchestrated by the G8 over the course of the last five decades, and have created the conditions for the rise of populist far-right movements as information ecosystems have become dominated by venture capital backed right wing media. As people are being subjected to increasing inequality, and democratic structures have been taken apart, anti-capitalists at the turn of the millennium rose up across the globe to oppose capitalist globalisation, anticipating the problems that we now can clearly see manifested in front of our eyes.

Fast forward to today, in planning for The World Transformed (TWT) Festival, scheduled to take place in Manchester in October 2025, we were thinking about transport to Manchester. In the pub afterwards the topic of the legendary anarchist train to Edinburgh (as part of the mobilisations against the G8 in Gleneagles on the 2nd-8th July 2005) came up and we began recounting the story of how it was organised to younger activists. We were both on this train—Jody as passenger, and Alessio as organiser. These experiences need to be re-told and re-explored as much of that period of late-90s/early-2000s anti-capitalism has faded. We captured some memories and the motivations from 2005. We include some of Jody's sketches from the train ride and our time in Scotland over the following days.

J: First, can you explain the political context in the UK in the 2000s?

A: Coming after the famously coined 'end of history' and with the ideological battles of the Cold War seemingly drawing to a close in 1989, between a decaying 'actually existing socialism' and a newly emboldened free market capitalism, new frontiers were being earmarked to be plundered. Structural Adjustment Programmes (SAP) were implemented by the IMF as a form of post-colonialism on already indebted global south and former post-Soviet nations, issuing dictates to liberalise (eg. privatise) their economies in return for loans. This conjuncture, far from signalling the end of history, was the beginning of a new phase.

Since 1999, from Seattle to Genoa, a diverse transnational social alliance of trade unions, civil society, and non-governmental organisations, along with more militant elements (anarchists, socialists, and eco-direct action movements), came together in an attempt to delegitimise the immense power of these summits, opposing not just the policies that would adversely affect billions of people, but also in opposition to the existence of capitalism itself.

That period of struggle produced new innovations in mobilisation, in street tactics and in activist technologies. It produced new possibilities, and emboldened a generation of activists and militants across the world. In Britain, movements emerged from their own history, from the defeats of the miners strike in 1984, from the autonomous rave culture, new age travellers and anti-roads protests throughout the 1990s, along with ecological and animal rights direct action, at the core was the ethics of DIY and self-organisation.

J: You were in a group called the W.O.M.B.L.E.S., can you tell us about it?

A: The W.O.M.B.L.E.S. was a group that formed to defend ourselves and others from the violence of the Met Police on Mayday 2001 in Central London. At the time, the threat of 'kettles' (where police surround and detain a large number of people for hours) and the rise in state repression during the wave of anti-capitalist protests was a big issue. Without being able to take the streets, it was hard for this movement to really exist. Most of us met whilst on a coach that I organised from London to Prague to attend the demonstrations against the World Bank and IMF on September 26th, 2001—a very seminal moment for many of us.

Our affinity group was formed on the coach to Prague. We decided to join the 'Yellow Bloc' on the big day of action, which was led by Ya Basta! and the Tute Bianche (White Overalls) movement from the occupied social centres in Italy. The 'colour blocs' was a tactic created during the organising meetings to embody the 'united in diversity' mantra that was prevalent. Each colour bloc—Red, Blue, Pink, Green, Yellow—would be led by a particular movement or alliances of movements, sharing tactical and sometimes political unity.

The tactics employed by the 'White Overalls' centered their bodies. The White Overalls, as the name suggests, wore white overalls padded with various soft cushions and helmets to protect themselves in an organised bloc that would attempt to push against police lines, often being met with police violence. The tactic was about producing 'dialogue through conflict', and the performance of that conflict to expose the violence of the state and the moral legitimacy of the protests.

We had been following the movements in Italy that had emerged in the 90s from the repression, a generation before, of the Autonomia movement of the 1970s and 80s. What inspired some of us was the intersection of new radical theory, militancy and this desire to challenge the state in such a public and open way. In particular, the militarisation of movements was seen as a political trap. So this move to demilitarise had been particularly important in the Italian context, after the armed conflicts by leftist groups with the state and the massive clampdowns that imprisoned and exiled the movement. Similarly, we were looking at the globally significant events in Chiapas, Mexico, and at the uprising led by the EZLN/Zapatista in 1994 against the introduction of the North American Free Trade Agreement (NAFTA). The EZLN's uprising began as a seizure of the capital, San Cristóbal de las Casas, but they also went through a similar demilitarisation phase early on and transitioned into an embedded social movement with aspirations of popular autonomy and horizontal self-governing structures.

In Britain, the New Labour government of Tony Blair, which had taken the country to war on falsified evidence, and was busy instituting public-private finance initiatives (PFI) under the 'Third-Way' doctrine, absolutely detested the left. For the Labourists, a Labour government was the pinnacle of working class empowerment and progress, so any challenges to that were seen as some sort of infantile disorder by middle-class students. The Met Police in particular was politicised to deal with the wave of confrontational protests that were led by anarchists, squatters and autonomous people. Even the 'socialist' Mayor of London at the time, Ken Livingstone, paid for

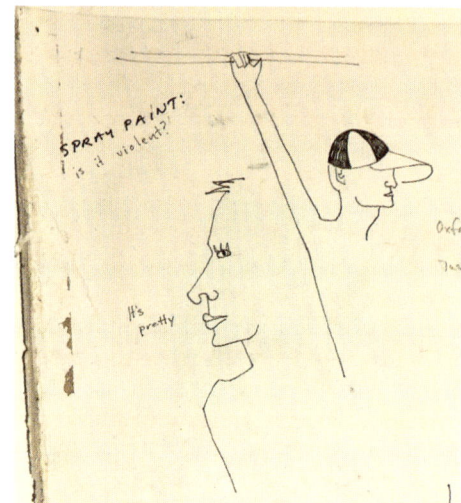

a full-page advert in three national newspapers urging people NOT to attend Mayday in 2001. Far from being new battles, it was the old ones that persisted between horizontal movements on one side, and state-backed top-down 'leftists' on the other. As the repression was being stepped up by the media, state and police, we felt in this context that these tactics of using 'padded blocs' would give confidence to people to stand up against this violence and not be scared off the streets. This is where we made our name. However, we only used the tactic a few times, and over the years developed into a wider political collective.

J: What discussions were happening at the time in the movement?

A: I remember there was this kind of reticence around going to Scotland. There was, at first, no enthusiasm for mobilising again. It felt like that whole period of, like, mobilisations that started in the late 90s had already kind of reached a point of exhaustion.

But for movements in Britain at that time this was the chance to actually host a big anti-summit protest and help us reinvigorate a movement that had been put on the defensive and was in decline. Remember, this was a tactic that some say had reached its limits in Genoa in 2001 (at the G8). That was the same year of the September 11th World Trade Center attacks—and defined a new global paradigm of war and the surveillance state. It was four years later and there was not much going on in the UK apart from ineffectual Stop the War demonstrations that suited the tradition of the left—with petitions, A to B marches and dull speeches. The spectacular dynamism of groups like Reclaim the Streets and mass creative actions had all but disappeared.

The institutional left, along with NGOs based in the global north, attempted to impose themselves on popular movements via the 'social forums', with the the World Social Forum (WSF) which was hosted in Porte Alegre in Brazil, and its European incarnation, the European Social Forum (ESF). WSF was a counter to the World Economic Forum (WEF) in Davos, a meeting of business and political elites. After the violence and murder of Carlo Guiliani at the Genoa protests in 2001, the ESF held a social forum in Florence, with the institutional backing of the mayor, which had something like 30,000 people in attendance, something huge. Tensions were emerging between the 'horizontalists' that saw these new bottom-up, popular movements that were self-organising and autonomous, and other actors; the institutional left, NGOs, and the old Leninist tendencies, or let's say the 'verticalists', that wanted to insert themselves as the leadership of the movement.

So 2005 felt very much like we wanted to revive ourselves as a movement, and so the autonomous DISSENT Network was formed to start making plans for Scotland.

J: What was the anarchist train to Scotland?

A: So the anarchist train to Scotland was for the occasion of bringing as many people as possible to attend the protests against the G8 in Gleneagles, Scotland in summer 2005. A few of us in the W.O.M.B.L.E.S. proposed the idea of a train at a big assembly of around 200 people in London which we had also helped co-organise.

J: The train to Scotland was anarchist-organised?

A: I mean we were anarchists, but in a wider sense we were an alliance of groups and individuals that had steered clear of the old trot left like the plague, the SWP in particular, and their cynical use of front-groups to take over movements. After all, it was the politics of direct

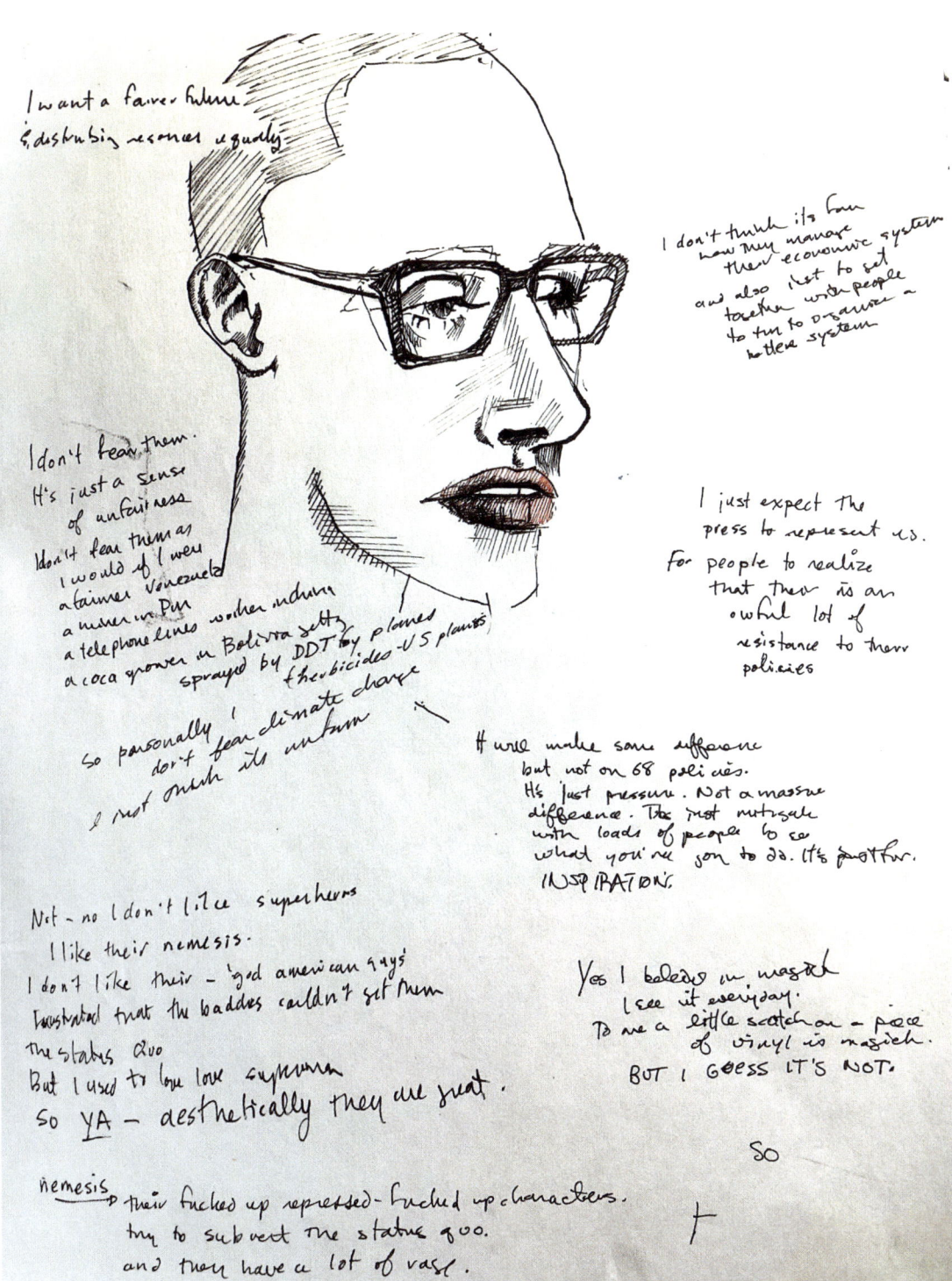

Rest in Power Nacho ♥

action, self-organisation and autonomy that created and energised these movements in the first place, and which was different from those other kinds of leftist protest movements. We saw that Globalise Resistance (a group that had emerged from the SWP) had announced they were organising a train from London to Edinburgh. We felt that we couldn't stand aside when it came to mobilising, because we had responsibility to the movements we've spent so much time and energy building on our own terms. I suppose it was also a case of the 'united in diversity' mantra and not purely sectarianism on our part, that led us to organise a train, and so we did.

J: So why did you rent a train instead of just renting a bus like everyone else?

A: We had attended protests in Europe where there were organised trains for activists. I was on a train from Milan to Naples back in March 2001 that was occupied by 1,000 activists. There was a negotiation between activists and the train company and cops, to carry the activists for free so as to exercise their political rights to protest. I had never seen

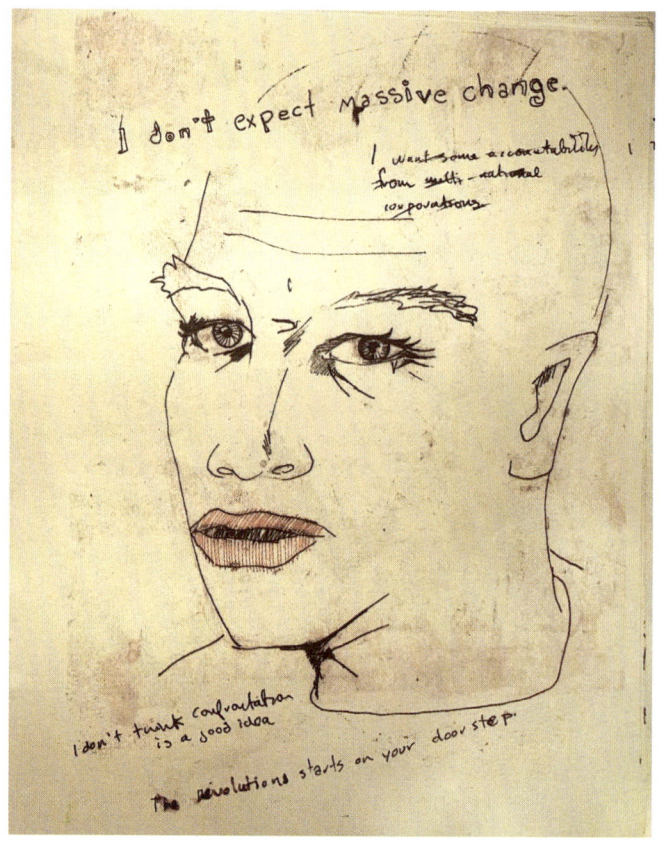

anything like this before—the coordination, the confidence, the political language. Perhaps in places like Italy at the time, because the level of social conflict was much higher historically, there was a kind of mutual respect around what it means for movements to demand stuff and the state to concede in such a way. During that whole journey I could see the kind of collectivity it produced in terms of people being together in such a space with large numbers. We fell in love with the idea and hoped that one day we would be able to do this at home.

Another reason we felt a bit off with using coaches was because a year earlier three coaches that we were involved in organising to take people to an action against the USAF base in Fairford were detained en route. Effectively around 150 of us were kidnapped by the cops and escorted back into London. It prevented us from attending the mass protests at the base, right at the time where B52 Bombers were being used to bomb Iraq. We were really cautious lest that happen again.

J: Did the police try to stop the train?

A: Well we knew it was a possibility, so we attempted to downplay what we were doing the best we could, and emphasise the broad range of participants. Our main aim was to get to Edinburgh and in one piece. Back then we didn't have smartphones in the same way we have now, so we relied on email lists, where we asked people to dress down like normal looking people—which no one, no one, did at all. So when we got to Kings Cross train station, we saw this huge kind of black bloc of people, with their backpacks, a lot wearing masks, and queuing on the platform by our specially-chartered train. There were lines of riot police and police forward intelligence teams, and all the senior cop commanders that knew us. When I got on the train and spoke with the train company rep, I was approached by a senior Met Police commander who reassured me that they won't prevent us from departing. It felt hugely empowering because, you know, we were there in this huge mob of people on this thing that we managed to make look quite legitimate, that was really public, without hiding who we were, that we somehow brought together, organised and paid for it—no big NGO's, no lefty parties or trade unions—just us. The cops couldn't do anything, where previously in other situations they would 'kettle' or attack us.

J: OK, let's go back to the train ride. So what was it like on the train?

A: Honestly, it was like a party. It was a nice vibe on the train because everyone was there for the same reason, from many different countries, it was very social. I remember people introducing themselves to each other, asking where they were from, joking and laughing, everyone had some common connection to the cause, you know. So it meant people were just striking up conversations all over the place.

We had come from occupying buildings, so this idea of entering a space and then 'subverting' it, and repurposing it was really attractive to us. We had a bar on the train that we stocked—some would say as a priority—with a sound system in one carriage. We started at about half eight in the morning and as soon as we could, we set the bar up and people started drinking. We didn't ask for permission. We had this train that we took a big risk in hiring and selling tickets for, and now we had it, we took it over. We had people organising workshops and sessions on the different carriages and announcing them, it was packed, and friendly and exciting to feel everyone's energy, that we were sharing this experience together. The train driver got into it as well, so he was announcing stuff for us on the train, it was all fairly good natured. It really felt like an autonomous space snaking through the countryside. We wanted to build that connectivity with each other on the way up there, something which you really can't do on a coach.

The train didn't stop, so we knew we'd have a good seven hours to compose ourselves, ready for the chaos we felt we were heading to. Having that pause, after so many months of organising, being able to chill out with comrades, this rag tag bunch of people, was one of those really special life-affirming experiences because, you know, we'd managed to create this thing out of pretty much nothing and there we were, actually doing it.

When we got to Edinburgh we were met by hundreds of activists that had swamped the station. There was a danger that the police might try to control us and stop and search people. It was quite a sight that the Anarchist Train from London, with over 800 people, was arriving, and I just remember this elation and applause we got when we arrived.

J: So what ended up happening in Scotland?

A: Well apart from the train, we had also called a mass assembly at the university there for the day after we arrived, and around 700 people turned up. We felt there wasn't enough coordination with the plan for blockades so we kind of filled that gap. After various rounds of

facilitating proposals, questions, shouting arguments and some commotion with a journalist being kicked out, we split into three areas: Stirling, Edinburgh & Glasgow. These were the three cities that would require blockades if we were to carry out our intention of disrupting the G8.

On the first day of action though, in Edinburgh, there was the 'Carnival for Full Employment', which descended into scuffles with the cops. I remember there were a lot of young Spanish anarchists that, as soon as they saw a line of cops, started smashing up pavement slabs and throwing rocks at them, in a very fearless way. They got into a massive ruck with the police, and more riot cops arrived. There were a number of arrests. All this tension was building up, through the media for days and weeks before, so something that was gonna be quite fluffy just quickly erupted and then got dispersed.

The main camp was in Stirling. There were around 5,000 people at it. They had self-organised neighbourhoods, organising food and waste removal with all kinds of necessities for big protest camps. There were presentations and assemblies and tactics and organising meetings and legal rights workshops. Our main group decided to head to Glasgow with around 200-300 people and stayed in a convergence centre. The aim was mass blockades for

the day of the Summit. Blockading delegates, blockading logistics, or blockading routes—basically that was the kind of plan. The massive draw of the Stirling camp meant that our numbers were down, with no real ability to pull anything off in Glasgow, so nothing really happened. A few of our comrades went out on bikes to reccy G8 delegates getting coaches, but we lost contact with them as they were arrested.

A small group of us decided to go up to Stirling and join the march to Gleneagles. When people left in the minibus, it got stopped by police in a planned raid. Around 100 riot cops appeared from behind the wall of this housing estate in Glasgow whilst the minibus was waiting at traffic lights and everyone got arrested. It turned out that the driver of the minibus was a long-term undercover cop that had infiltrated our movement.

For those of us that weren't arrested and still stuck in Glasgow, all we could do was follow the news and the reports being published by the Indymedia activists. In Sterling there were black bloc anarchists charging police and being charged on the motorway towards Gleneagles. Activists pulling down fences and, most bizarrely, British Army Chinook helicopters landing with dozens of Met riot cops inside.

J: Stirling was the start of Climate Camp for a lot of people?

A: Exactly. The Climate Camps (note: the UK Camps for Climate Action 2006-2010 were a series of large scale protest camps near large fossil fuel burning infrastructure) concept began at Stirling, and even the tactics of leading multiple blocs of people in different directions, termed the 'five finger tactic' because they were 5 different marches, also inspired the Ende Gelände camps in Germany a decade later.

So this mobilisation was the start of something new. There was this thing where people were asking before Scotland 'What's the point of anti-summit mobilisations when what happens is that you get increased repression?' The only outcome seemed to be that you get activists burnt out for years, and nothing much else. The protests were spectacular, don't get me wrong, but what had originally inspired thousands of us to get involved had reached a limit. There was a growing awareness that we wanted to move away from just these big anti-summit protests, whilst still maintaining the scale of them.

Many of the activists were coming from more ecological perspectives, and the prevention of the impending climate catastrophe was a priority. So one main aim was to try out the organising of a large camp to host activists during the summit, to build up the necessary infrastructure and knowledge to do this at scale. The Stirling camp, called the 'Hori-zone', in reference to the horizontality of the politics, was to become the precursor of the 'Climate Camps'. This was roughly where a large portion of that movement was heading anyway, and the Climate Camp UK started the following year to oppose Drax, a coal-fired power station, in North Yorkshire.

J: And then the bombings happened in London?.

A: Yes. This was the spectre that was haunting Europe with terrorism and the Al-Qaeda inspired attacks that hit London buses on July 7th, 2005. It was very close to home because it was in areas that we lived in, like Camden, Hackney and Whitechapel. In Glasgow, we were waiting for our comrades who were arrested in the minibus, and we were in a pub when we saw the news, on live TV, these bombs happening across London and it just got kind of surreal...very much like watching the planes hit the World Trade Center, on repeat, but a horror more close to home for us.

So at the same time when we were doing these creative, spectacular actions, challenging these big global institutions, and really gaining momentum to advance social justice agendas, we witnessed the emergence of this new form of spectacular Al-Qaeda terrorism, aimed at ordinary people. The surrealism of that moment was that we knew we were both agents of social change and spectators of terrorism in our communities. We had the G8 in Gleneagles and this massive repression, with police arresting our friends—and then you had these terrorists killing innocent people in the neighbourhoods where some of us lived in London.

The next day, we were all heading back to London, back to Kings Cross Station. We were quite subdued, it was a come down, the exhaustion, and the adrenaline fatigue and coming from a euphoric kind of hopefulness up in Scotland. We've managed to pull this thing off and brought so many people to Scotland—and people managed to burst through fences. Was it a victory, well, a minor one. And then coming back to the reality of this horrible terrorist attack.

J: What for you was the legacy of this 2005 G8 Gleneagles Scotland mobilisation?

A: It was the start of the Climate Camps. These inspired a new generation of activists. The movements were broadening and we could see they were also professionalising. With NGO money and activists being recruited into them, more could be done, but at the cost of changing the character of the movement.

It later transpired, as the financial crisis was beginning to hit in 2007/8, that the movements were heavily infiltrated by the state. By the time the first exposure came with Mark Kennedy in 2009, it impacted the confidence of people, a lot of fractures emerged, which in my mind caused a generational discontinuity, but for others it was a convenient departure point. After 5, 10, 15 years of struggles, they decided to do other things, and people were burning out.

There was definitely a point where things disintegrated internationally—perhaps at the onset of the financial crisis. A lot of movements became a lot more inward looking because they were defending their livelihoods against the attacks from their own 'national capital'. We went from fighting against structural adjustment programmes in the global south, and World Bank and IMF summits forcing austerity on developing nations, to the very same institutions doing their own structural adjustments and austerity measures in the imperial core. The wave of austerity protests, that were patchy, only really began by the unforeseen explosion of the 2010 student movement.

For me the legacy of the 2025 Gleneagles mobilisation lives on in different ways, but it has suffered, and has failed to be recognised with the importance it deserves. With the decline of transnational movements, there is a rise of national, far-right ones. It's important to remember our own history. It was anti-capitalists, workers and peasant farmers and indigenous activists in the global south that led the fight against capitalist globalisation, against things like the World Economic Forum (WEF), the expansion of the EU, of NATO and for freedom of movement for all. It was a movement that named its enemy, Global Capitalism, that distanced itself from the failed 'state communist' experiments of the twentieth century, and attempted to chart a route to a new political horizon. It's vital that we pick up this legacy, and begin again on a new journey.

How material conditions make our refusal an option, but not if we only offer abstractions. Why the right is able to weaponise that refusal when we don't offer concrete options.

In *Haunted by the Ghost of the Collective Subject*, we explored the reasons why left-wing ideas aren't put into practice, even though they are popular. We argued that this happens when the social infrastructure that would allow people to see themselves as part of a wider collective project is missing in our society. This article instead focuses on understanding why the right is gaining support even though their ideas are really unpopular.

The political and economic conditions, and the naked corruption that developed under Tory austerity for 14 years, have stoked discontent with politicians and state institutions to a level never seen before. Keir Starmer's new 'Tory-Lite' government was almost immediately embroiled in scandals over the £100K of freebies he received while he was busy cutting winter fuel payments for pensioners. Only about 10% of people said they trusted politicians in the most recent Office of National Statistics (ONS) 'Trust in Government' survey; and in the latest Ipsos Veracity Index, that figure was just 2% for people aged 25-34. We've been saying this stuff for years, right? Politicians are only in it for themselves and we need to tear the whole system down… But now it's the left that is being seen as the defender of the status quo and the right that's seen as an agent of change.

Meanwhile, the dire housing situation and cost of living crisis created conditions that might have been expected to lead to widespread opportunities for left-wing ideas to spark refusal. However, this is simply not happening on anything like the scale it did in the past. The ONS survey also shows that the number of people who see the rising cost of living as their most important political issue is more than double the number of those who said it was immigration. But it's immigration that fuels the rage that brings people out on the street, not prices. The old assumption that material conditions as bad as this will

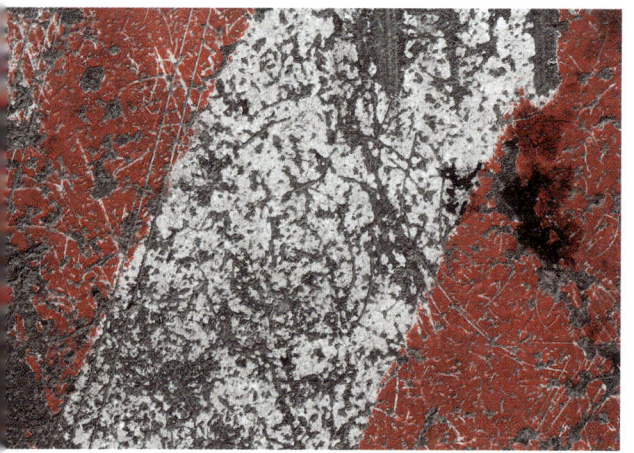

lead people to automatically (spontaneously) move to the left has been proven incorrect, at least in the UK. Instead, it is the right that has stepped in and gained strength amongst constituencies that were once strongholds of left radicalism, weaponising refusal for their own purposes in the process.

One particularly notable aspect of this moment is that at the very same time, the left is failing to gain support for popular ideas. By contrast, the right is winning support for unpopular ideas. For fuck's sake, people who idolise Hitler are more successful at building their movement than we are! In the aftermath of the July 2024 riots, we were through the looking glass like Alice in Wonderland, to the point where the reactionary right were the ones fighting the cops and burning police cars, while the police praised anti-fascists for maintaining the peace. Racism is so unpopular that even racists don't want to be labelled as racist, yet mobs of people have been strolling through the streets attacking the homes and cars of people thought to be immigrants.

While there are a number of factors driving all this, we are specifically looking at the way the narratives of the far right are in the ascendancy and the messages of the left aren't achieving the same level of popularity. To understand what's happening, let's briefly look at the current situation in the UK, then show how the far right uses short-cuts to win support for their ideas; and how this is exacerbated when we stop centering class in our language. Then we'll show why the left misses its mark(s) and provide some strategies we can try out to be more effective.

1. Things Are Shit

'To put it bluntly: if the far right has managed to mobilize the anti-systemic feelings of people, it is because those sentiments exist. It is only because many people sense that there is something profoundly wrong about the existing economic and political system that the far right's message can take hold.'

Rodrigo Nunez, Are we in Denial about Denial?

Rodrigo Nunez provides the starting point for all this. Money is tight, jobs are precarious, NHS waiting lists are too long, housing is a nightmare. There are a lot of very angry people who don't want to be fobbed off. All these things are real, not imagined. For many working class people, our lives are chaotic and very stressful. 'Insecurity is the defining characteristic of our economic era,' according to a 2022 report by the Autonomy Institute. The world's ten richest men more than doubled their wealth during the Covid pandemic, while simultaneously over 160 million other people were forced into poverty. The perceived unfairness of lockdown continues to have a far-reaching impact on society. Working class people are moving away from a collective strategy of organising to an increasingly individualised strategy of hustling.

DELETE, *Untitled*

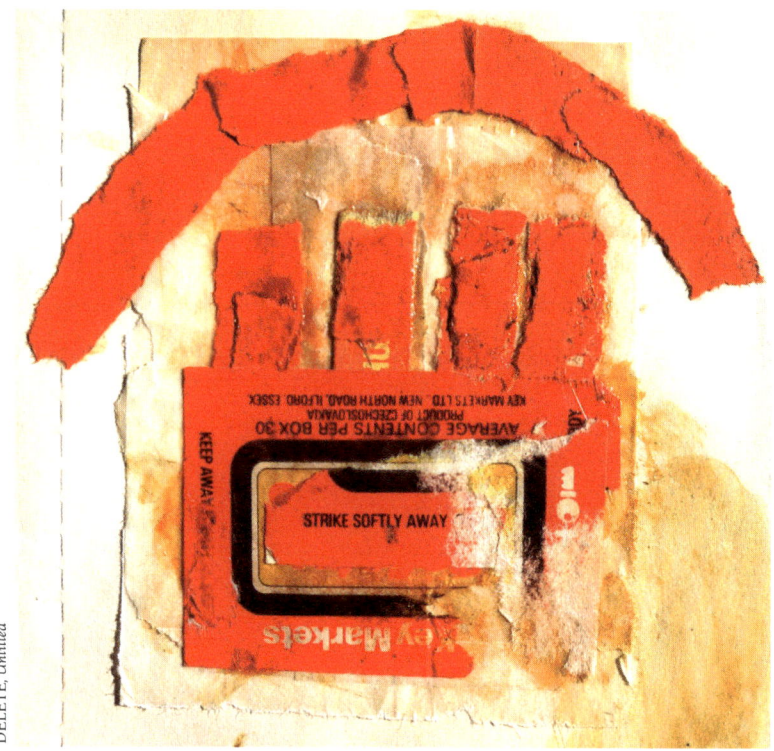

DELETE, Untitled

Although billionaires themselves live a rarified existence far from our reality, the vast inequality is constantly being shoved in our faces. Researchers have found that economic inequality like this has a measurable impact on support for the far right (e.g. 'How Does Income Inequality Affect the Support for Populist Parties?' *Journal of European Public Policy* 2021). Everything is broken. People sense the increasing fragility of society, and feel something brewing on the horizon.

Displacement

Class struggle is still our lived experience, in longer working hours, wages losing value, and loss of job security. On the other hand, class struggle has ceased to be the way people identify their conditions, their precarity, or their response to any of this. When you remove class from this chaotic living situation, without removing the problems that you're enduring, you're still going to need to find a reason why all this is happening to you. That search for a reason (blame) can lead to a displacement of struggle— we end up pitting self-employed workers against council workers or taxpayers against 'benefit cheats', commuters against environmentalists. The far right's response is to speak to that anxiety and also to displace it very clearly and specifically onto migrants, feminists, gender, and wokeness.

'It is not that people are unaware of the gigantic inequalities that determine life, but that the language of class often doesn't hit home, viscerally, as an explanation. And what it means when class is a less structurally plausible explanation [is that] patient class hate is less resonant than the reactive emotions borne of helplessness'
   Richard Seymour, Literally Nothing: Sick in the Heart of Working Class Life

There is a genuine and widespread anger about unfairness, and a visceral contempt for corrupt politicians because 'they're all the same'. Distrust of politicians has gradually become distrust in politics in general, and often now includes anyone who even talks about politics. This means that overtly ideological messages are often written off, but appeals to 'common sense' can be warmly received. This is of course despite common sense being as ideological as anything else (especially when its source is the Daily Mail). In Donald Trump's 2024 election victory speech, one of his core messages was that Republicans are 'the party of common sense'. The use of common sense in this

Peter Newell, *Howled for Hours*

way becomes a 'fog of war' that hides the differing and conflicting material interests and political positions that explain our lives, preventing a clear analysis and making it easier for the far right to find a way to place the blame on the things that they always wanted to place the blame on in the first place.

'What starts as sadness, anxiety, grief, worry is carefully manipulated into political rage.'

Michael Kimmel, Angry White Men

Short cuts and hostile environments

A big reason for the success of the far right's message comes down to the way that they avoid actually talking about the complex causes of our daily misery. They deliberately avoid abstractions like capitalism or class. They invent easier and more pressing problems, with easier solutions—whilst always acknowledging how bad things are. The concern of the right for our everyday experience is opportunistic and insincere, and they have no intention of addressing its real underlying causes.

For example, while the right's 'Save Our Kids' campaigns tap into widespread public revulsion about child abuse, they plainly could not care less about any of the victims, have nothing to offer as a way to actually protect children, nor have they got anything to say about the overwhelming majority of cases which aren't perpetrated by what they label as 'Muslim gangs'. The right's only interest in the victims of child abuse is to further use them as tools for anti-immigration propaganda, which they have been able to do in a highly effective manner. The sudden interest in women's rights of people like Farage when they apply to the hijab, is obviously not concerned with addressing the role of patriarchy or the profound sexism which allows men to think that women and girls can be brutally commodified. Their manufactured concern sits in stark contrast to the domestic abuse and misogyny which are rife in right-wing organisations.

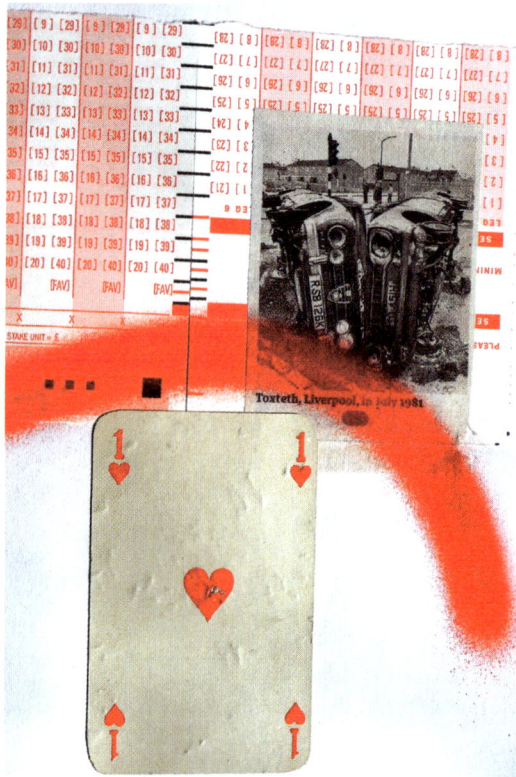

DELETE, Untitled

So, they have easy answers (which aren't actually solutions to anything at all) which provide concrete examples of what they identify as your problem and/or your enemy. The far right recruit people who are (rightly) pissed off with the state of society, by offering short cuts that they say will fix their problems. Obviously, the issues are more complicated, nuanced, and difficult than the right allows for. Meanwhile the left might address those complexities but frequently doesn't have a resonating message to offer as an alternative, allowing the right to fill the political void by creating their targets of hate.

This strategy is straight out of the playbook of Carl Schmitt, an influential Nazi philosopher known as the 'Crown Jurist of the Third Reich'. His idea was to start by choosing an enemy, and then set yourself up in opposition to 'the Other'. According to Schmitt, it doesn't even particularly matter who the 'Other' is, although in British political history it has almost always been racialised, which makes it so easy for transparent 5-star-hotel grifters like Tommy Robinson and Nigel Farage to point at immigrants and say something like, 'They've been given your homes, your jobs, your healthcare and your services. They're not like you. They are dangerous. They are your enemies. They're killing your children'. And if you, your family, your mates, your kids have suffered the ravages of austerity, shitty housing, the cost of living crisis and years of propaganda blaming that Other (including both Labour and Tory official government policy of creating a 'hostile environment'), you can easily become the dry wood that gets used to start a very nasty fire. Add to this the decision of the government to consistently house asylum seekers in the poorest working class communities, and the manufactured struggle over resources is made intentionally obvious to all.

People aren't stupid, but you can't ignore the impact of this relentless drumbeat of xenophobia—which underscores almost every other social discourse—on angry ('white') working class people who are alienated, criminalised, confused and who have lost any sense of being valued or heard. While demands raised about material and social conditions are explicitly and intentionally ignored, the way that mainstream politicians centre the 'white' working class to gain their electoral support feeds a sense that their voices in particular ought to be heard, and creates a sense of aggrieved entitlement when they are repeatedly not.

Plausible Deniability

Working class people are well aware of what the rich are doing to us but they rarely have opportunities to face off against them. Under such conditions it becomes far easier to seek revenge for this situation by targeting 'immigrants' and 'middle class do-gooders' instead. The habit of the far right to further demonise these enemies as terrorists and nonces makes it easy for their audience to dismiss everything they might have to say.

Beyond their racism, the far right has no programme or policy. They will talk about migrants, Muslims, hotels, grooming gangs. But they have no solutions, not even basic social reorganisation. Nigel Farage's Reform Party started off by connecting with voters through a grab bag of the material issues that really matter to people, before cynically offering a ban on immigration as a plausible-sounding solution. They had to reverse-engineer immigration as the reason for all of our problems because

DELETE, Untitled

Odilon Redon, *Misty Outline of a Human Figure*

in reality they support the actual cause of the problems (and often want to make it worse).

Destroying our capacity to organise (specifically by trampling over trade union rights and creating a 'flexible labour market') is integral to the right's programme. Like many other right-wing grifters, Reform are happy to champion the working class when it is useful to them but definitely not when workers assert their collective power to defend their interests. From housing to education and health, from benefits to childcare, from pay to conditions, critics of immigration often support policies deeply detrimental to the working class and hide it behind a game of 'blame the foreigner'.

When you're a right-wing, pro-austerity, NHS-privatising, neoliberal politician it's very important to point the blame as far away as possible from the political and economic decisions that have caused the mess we all have to live in. And when all you have are racist answers it doesn't really matter what the question is.

DELETE, Untitled

The Dog Whistle of Nostalgia

These short cuts, the common sense truisms, and the targets of blame, are all illuminated in the warm glow of a kind of reactionary nostalgia to 'make Britain once again what it never was', which is a particularly useful means of helping us to forget that it was always shit for people like us. They provide a robust and relatable answer to the question, 'why are things so bad now, when they never used to be?', but that question itself is an attempt to throw a blanket of amnesia over the past.

So, things are bad and we know it. People are angry about it. In the past this might have been expressed through political activity, industrial action and protests. Through refusal, the natural home of the left. But now, that political activity no longer feels relevant to our lives, and unions are seen as something for other people. Even enormous protest marches achieve very little. In the context of all of this, just why is it that these anti-systemic feelings are being so successfully harnessed by the right instead? Because things are so bad that there's no way out. Because they are anti-systemic politics for people <u>who don't think the system will change</u>.

'The painful reality is that the story that the far right tells effectively makes more sense to a lot of people than whatever the left is saying. This is because the far right's story corresponds more clearly to the world as most people encounter it on a daily basis; it resonates with lived experience. For a lot of people, being told that life is a series of dark trade-offs in a deadly struggle over finite resources does not sound far-fetched at all. What is more, it resonates with the disciplining effect that these experiences actually have: the deeply entrenched feeling that this is all that is possible, that the fundamental facts of how we live could not change. By locating the source of the problem in the misappropriation of resources by various others and the solution in a fight to exclude those others from access to resources, the far right tells a story that is well adapted to a world in which inequality grows, resources decline, and those at the bottom have to compete for increasingly meagre scraps.'

Rodrigo Nunez, Are we in Denial about Denial?

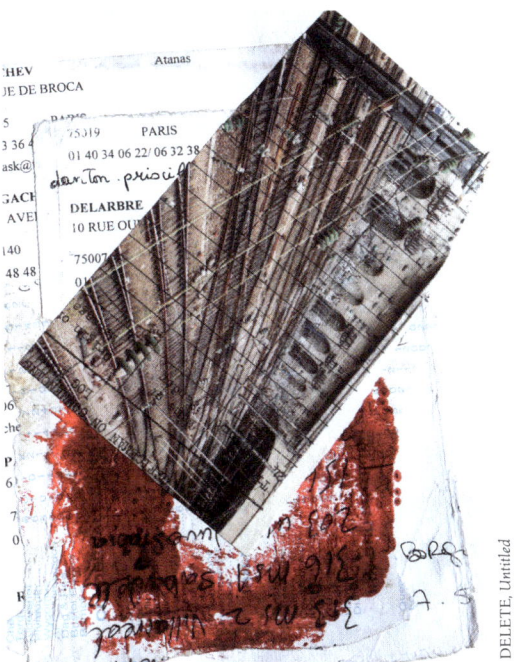

DELETE, Untitled

2. Racialised workers and aggrieved entitlement

'In order to belong to this "working class", whiteness is indispensable, while any specific relation to the means of production is optional at best.'
Alberto Toscano, Notes on Late Fascism

Much of the media commentary about the causes of the riots of July 2024 has focused on the 'white working class' who are uniquely marginalised, disenfranchised and left behind. The far right was clearly deeply involved in these riots, having organised multiple similar demonstrations outside hotels housing asylum seekers and an earlier riot in Knowsley in 2023. But at the same time, many angry working class people who were not part of any right-wing organisation were also out on the street throwing rocks at the police. These people are now all being lumped in with the far right as thugs and racists. It seems clear that among those arrested after the riots, there were plenty of people who were neither fascists or racists, but local people having a go when a riot started on their doorstep—many of them drunk. Of course, others were clearly racist shitbags, and it appears that among this group many had travelled some distance and had good jobs, well paid jobs, and were not the archetypal poor and marginalised at all (although they certainly weren't middle class).

But before we go any further, let's pause for a moment to consider a surreal fantasy world where it is such a thing as a 'white working class' that gets the shitty end of the stick and it is Black people and specifically Muslims who get favourable treatment from cops, employers, and public services. Where fleeing war and persecution to find yourself stuck living three or four-up with strangers in a crap hotel room for months on end and existing on pennies, isn't a nightmare at all, but a luxury...

Negative Solidarity

The point being that when we talk about these communities being forgotten and left behind, we act as if any other part of the working class has not been forgotten or left behind. It's important that we treat this racialised 'white working class' community not as separate and unique but as a dramatic manifestation of the precarity that defines working class life more generally. Because otherwise, by talking in these terms, we accept the fictitious racial unity invented by fascists, and double down on it. We unintentionally contribute to their project of polarisation.

> 'The new fascisms conquered political hegemony above all by designating the immigrant, the Muslim as the enemy. The political polarizations are, through racism, reconfigured into a phantasmal but "real" people that takes a form and an identity by being set against a common enemy.'
>
> *Maurizio Lazzarato, Capital Hates Everyone*

To the extent that 'white' workers have been racialised, this is only really in terms of what they are 'not'. This magnifies even more the value of othering migrants–because only through the negative solidarity of polarising one part of the working class against some fabricated 'Other' can the right create and build coherence and meaning, can create a white working class. In reality, there is no such thing as a homogenous 'white working class' culture. And migrant peoples, whether they arrive on a small boat or not, are usually working class people too.

Charles Raymond Macaulay, *Clubbed Him To The Earth*

DELETE, Untitled

Identity

Some sections of the working class have become open to these identitarian arguments because of the feeling that much of the left has favoured the politics of identity while distancing themselves from the politics of class. This general shift towards identitarian politics without class politics has created a discursive situation that the right has managed to take great advantage of. As the Labour Party has abandoned its traditional working class voters, leaving many feeling ignored and voiceless, some people in former Labour constituencies have turned to the language of whiteness to find a social anchor. The right have been able to tap into this racialised section of the working class, using the splits and splintering made by neoliberalism and pushing people to see those beyond the boundaries of their identity as threats. They tell lies (about Muslims and refugees) that people were already primed to listen to.

This focus on whiteness, not class, feeds into a sense of aggrieved entitlement in post-industrial towns and cities, shifting the blame for the situation from the ruling class who smashed industrial production, onto immigrants who are being exploited in the precarious and badly-paid jobs that came afterwards. Racism is a product of the political economy.

Viewing this moment through the lens of 'identity' or 'culture', and not class, allows the right to expand the kind of socially constructed anger that negative solidarity depends on, the sense that you have been wronged and the people who have wronged you are to be found, at least in part, among those who are beneath you in some kind of social hierarchy. The sense that 'we' have had what is 'rightfully ours' taken away by 'them' (politicians) and given to the Other (migrants).

Resentment and Revenge

'The resentment bred by class experience can be dangerous. It can be a demoralising, self-destructive emotion. It has been said that resentment is like swallowing poison and waiting for the other chap to die. It can also be profoundly reactionary.'
Richard Seymour, Literally Nothing: Sick in the Heart of Working Class Life

Richard Seymour talks here about resentment, but perhaps this explosion of anger is more like revenge. Like the Brexit revenge, a Fuck You to the system, even though it was largely an act of self-harm to the very people who voted for it. The far right is stoking an instinct for revenge on the 'woke', the middle class professionals and managers, the ones that are in our faces—not the abstract rich or the ruling class. The people who ignore us, marginalise, abandon us. For people like Farage and Lee Anderson, this is their revenge on the Establishment, and on mainstream politicians, who they want to push aside so they can take their place.

In response to this identitarian movement that makes 'white' the most important aspect, it's crucial that we don't accept the racialised frame 'white working class'. It's a class division which only exists in opposition to other groups, and without

this negative definition there is nothing there to be seen. But if we start from this false premise that there is a 'white working class' there is no way through to political class consciousness (which is exactly what the right wants). In the end, intra-class antagonism can only benefit the rich.

In this far-right vision of politics, frustrations and fears work to reinforce divisions and hierarchies between racialised groups. The opposite of all this is our politics of solidarity, that takes as a starting point that we are all, white, Black, immigrant, gendered or not, waged and unwaged, workers. All of us exploited.

Unknown Artist, *Central Telephone Exchange*

3. Failure to connect

As mentioned earlier, Things Are Shit. Objectively and materially speaking, this is not because of immigration. It's also not because of overpopulation. Or 'Cancel Culture'. Or the EU. Far more than anything else, it's the result of 15 years of Tory austerity that has gutted public services in every corner of the country. As a quick reminder:

There's a cost of living crisis, but the energy companies and supermarkets are making record profits (in 2022 Shell reported its highest profits in 115 years, British Gas owners Centrica more than trebled their profits in 2023, and in 2024 UK supermarkets made a 97% increase in profits for the year when food price inflation reached 19.1%).

There's a housing crisis, but how can there be a housing shortage when there are over 1 million empty homes in England? When landlords financialise our homes to generate unearned income. There has been a deliberate government policy of property value inflation in order to make a collapsing economy feel better. Social housing availability has been hammered by the Right to Buy. One of the three major companies that the government pays to provide accommodation for asylum seekers (Clearsprings Ready Homes) made £90 million in profit from the scheme in 2024.

Wages are stagnant because of the decline of union power, along with the rise of self-employment and Uberisation. Study after study shows that immigration doesn't affect wages. Who cuts our pay? Well, it's the boss, not other workers. The NHS struggles with massive waiting lists, shortages of GPs and dentists because of a decade of underinvestment, privatisation and cuts (and would collapse overnight without the 384,000 non-white workers that make up 24% of the NHS workforce).

Shake it Off

Everywhere people are angry about all these things—the cost of living, the effects of austerity on public services, the improbability of affording a house, a lack of job opportunities, and they are filled with the overriding feeling that politicians need 'a good shake-up'. The blame for most of these problems is frequently and conveniently placed on immigration. The language of the right has an emotional grip on the national conversation in a way that we do not. The fragmentation and alienation that prevents people from believing that our ideas aren't viable, also feed neatly into the far right's story of competition over dwindling resources.

Unknown Artist, *A Butcher Shop*

Le siège de Paris. —Une boucherie spéciale au marché Saint-Germain.

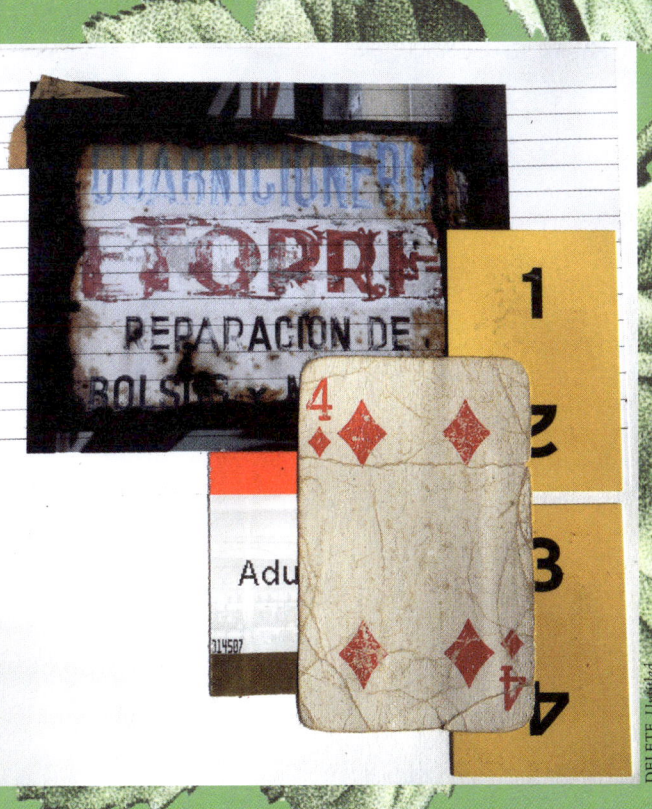

DELETE, Untitled

Usually, the left tends to counter these arguments with either facts or abstractions. We can reel off a load of data to prove our point but statistics alone don't persuade in the arena of emotion. In politics truth often holds very little importance, and the right's most successful messages are often full of lies, told with such confidence and clarity that it can make the falsehoods irrelevant. The left can always offer great big abstract visions of the future. We have some ideas to share but often no immediate or practical way to turn them into action. We put ineffectual stickers about socialism on lamp posts, which neither motivate working class people, spark joy at collective possibilities nor strike fear into the rich. As a comparison, when the right plaster an area with their hateful stickers it can generate enough menace to make whole communities uneasy.

The left can sometimes fall into the habit of relating to the working class as an abstract category rather than a concrete social body of real people (you, your family, your mates, your kids...), when we must never forget that class is a social relationship. The left's problems are not restricted to political messaging, but our messaging is part of the problem.

Big words and big ideas

Even just talking about 'the Left' as if it is one coherent movement is problematic. Any definition would encompass everything from rag-tag anarchists to doctrinaire state socialists, with the more radical elements often subsumed within the liberal social democratic currents, as if there's no difference between us all or as if we're all fellow travellers of Starmer's Labour Party. We don't all put ineffectual stickers about socialism on lamp posts!

This discussion is aimed at our comrades on the revolutionary anti-capitalist left, but we can't ignore the broad political habitat that we operate in, or the political ecology within it.

It's absolutely not the intention of this article that anyone should take this criticism of the left personally. We are talking in general terms across the whole milieu (including Plan C) and however you want to define it, there's no part of the left that is significantly growing/seizing power/succeeding. While all over the world, that's exactly what the right is doing. We hope that it is obvious that we aren't saying that there isn't anyone, anywhere, on the left that is managing to do anything worthwhile. But taken as a whole, it is surely clear that our movement/current/politics are failing to achieve working class support where we would historically expect (and need) to do so, given the material conditions we are all experiencing.

Passion and rage

All over the country base unions, tenants unions, and local grassroots groups are doing fantastic things, and they are definitely having an impact on their members and communities, but it's all comparatively small scale and contained. The talking points of the left are not being repeated in pubs and workplaces in the same easy way that the right's talking points currently are. There are a lot of reasons for that of course, but the left often doesn't help itself because of the way we talk about our politics.

We will talk about how the power of a violent abstraction (Capitalism) runs people's lives, neoliberal marketisation of society, equality, austerity, freedom of movement (social relationships!). All of it is too abstract, too theoretical and very hard to relate to lived experience. And besides, is there any point in having a rational argument about facts with people who don't care? Especially given the way

they've been ignored by the left, other than as an abstract part of the class we consider so important for revolution. There is a sense that as a movement (current) the left isn't angry (enough), isn't able to satisfy people's genuine and powerful grievances, doesn't have anything to offer pissed off workers as a way to get revenge. We are seen to have big words and big ideas instead of passion and rage.

We're not suggesting that the left shouldn't discuss or explore abstract ideas, nor that working class people outside of left organisations aren't able to understand abstract ideas. In the end, however, all political ideas and concepts are abstract, until someone punches you in the face. Yes, abstract concepts are worth fighting for—but in an effective way. Our point is a simple and practical one, that the left needs to communicate our messages in a more effective and relevant way; and that includes very much what we do, just as much as what we say.

DELETE, *Untitled*

4. What can we do?

'The philosophers have only interpreted the world in various ways; the point, however, is to change it.'
Karl Marx, 11th Thesis on Feuerbach

If we as the left want to make inroads into the current political and economic terrain, we will need to do a few things differently to make that happen. We need to learn from our mistakes and change the way that we do things. There are also lessons to be learned by understanding the success of the far right, without copying their poisonous political strategy.

If faith in the state and/or its institutions is at the lowest level ever, why aren't we getting any success from that situation? We sometimes find ourselves arguing that they're not 'all the same' (for example when talking about the value of getting rid of the Tories after 14 years), and in a context where nuance is next to impossible, we can become associated with the corrupt and selfish politicians that we also despise as much as anyone else. Then we're all the same. We must have a very clear separation between what we're doing and what (all) politicians are doing. We have to demonstrate difference. The distrust of institutions should allow space to build counter power (through counter institutions) but that's only going to work if it is based on practical day-to-day work.

Whose Streets?

'Antifascism is a century-old tradition now. It's a politics of memory and meaning that are fading from this world. It's perhaps too idealistic, too abstract and airy, and not focused enough on practical issues'
John Ganz, I Hope I'm Wrong

If we attack everyone pulled into the activity of the far right as racists, it will be totally counter-productive. Without diminishing the importance of fighting racism, there is an urgent need to differentiate between far right activists and their organisations, and the working class people being swept along in their current. As the fascist ecosystem grows it has a kind of gravitational pull of validity and relevance to everyday problems. Not everyone caught up in all this is a racist. We need to split working class people from the fascists and fill the void left behind with our own activity. If we're successful with this, eventually it will result in a confrontation—one which we will have to win.

So of course, it's vital that we maintain and grow a combative anti-fascism to challenge far-right street activity but we need to be on the ground daily to have an impact beyond a few punch-ups (which in many parts of the country we would probably lose right now anyway). In the past we could usually rely on the constant internal battles between the giant, fragile egos leading fascist groups (or their relentless desire to make money off each other) to apply self-inflicted damage to their movement. But it seems like nowadays there is enough money being pumped into the far right from millionaires overseas to stabilise that side of things. Their street movement is strong, and we need to take that side of things very seriously.

Language matters

If the far right is successfully using a certain kind of language, we can't ignore the success of that or how much it highlights that our own language is not hitting home. We need to shrink the gap between the right's concrete targets and our abstract ideas. We need to be clear where it matters; we need to be making concrete demands rather than vague slogans. If Clearsprings is making gigantic profits from asylum accommodation, and their boss Graham King is worth £750 million, why aren't they being targeted for rinsing the taxpayers, instead of the desperately impoverished refugees on the receiving end of their threadbare 'hospitality'? We need to be explicit about what we want and how we're going to get it.

However, the purpose of this discussion isn't to be prescriptive about political messages, beyond the request that we very much need to move way beyond the kind of Father Ted 'Down With This Sort Of Thing' slogans, like 'Stop The Cuts' or 'Fight Racism'. This is a plea for strategy change, rather than a blueprint for a media campaign. We're pointing a way forward that we can figure out together. Every community, every struggle needs its own messages. We need to explore the possibilities of a left populism that directly ties the billionaires that are playing with our lives, with the consequences of their games. A bit of joined-up thinking to tie the ephemeral rich directly to the impact of their decisions on us as workers, tenants or consumers. The huge groundswell of support for Luigi Mangione shows how quickly the most entrenched conversations can be turned by effective action.

Making connections

If we're talking about 'class warfare', 'the rich' or 'the elite', in an abstract sense, these can instead be made explicit and material. It's not so hard to identify enemies such as landlords or estate agents that have a direct negative impact on our lives (and our pockets). Of course, this takes our aim away from the ruling class and trains it on their middle class enablers, but if we are able to connect our local issues with what is causing them, this can also be effective. The 'Don't Pay' energy bill strike campaign was a notable example of how this messaging can gain a wide reach beyond the organised left.

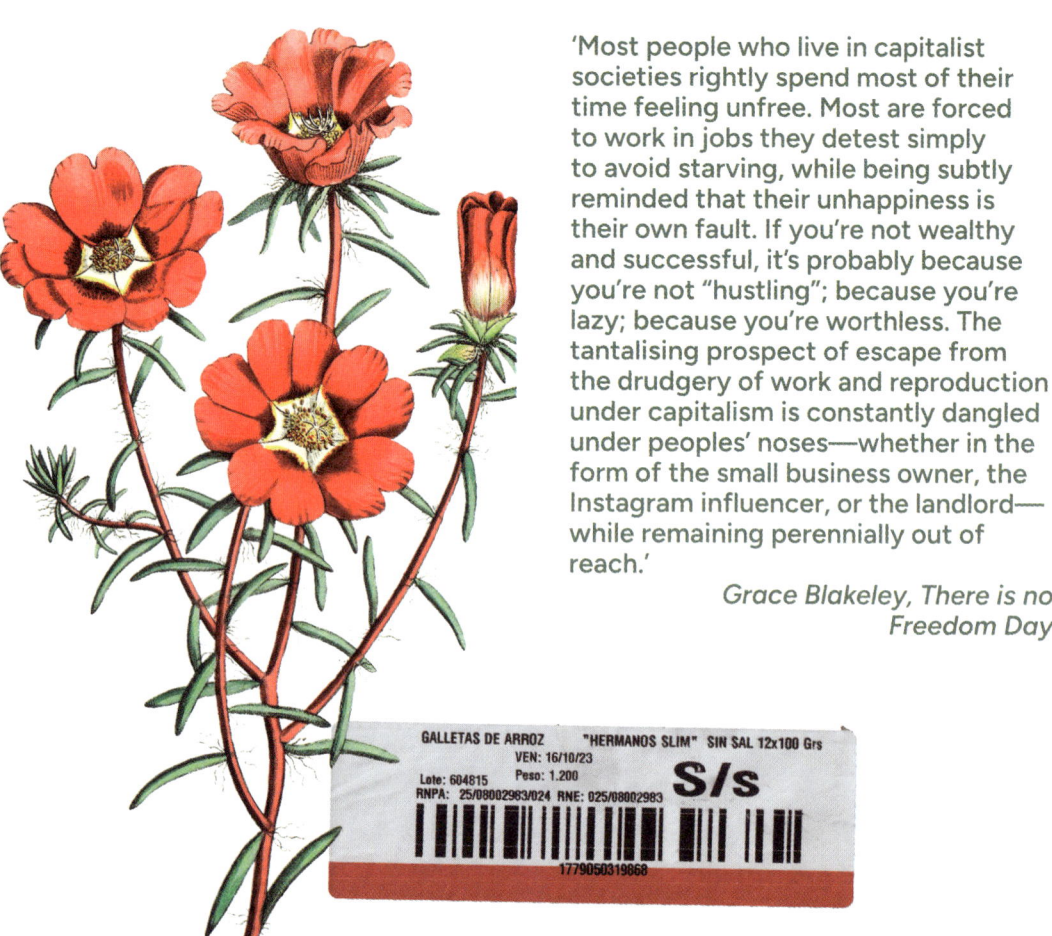

'Most people who live in capitalist societies rightly spend most of their time feeling unfree. Most are forced to work in jobs they detest simply to avoid starving, while being subtly reminded that their unhappiness is their own fault. If you're not wealthy and successful, it's probably because you're not "hustling"; because you're lazy; because you're worthless. The tantalising prospect of escape from the drudgery of work and reproduction under capitalism is constantly dangled under peoples' noses—whether in the form of the small business owner, the Instagram influencer, or the landlord—while remaining perennially out of reach.'

Grace Blakeley, There is no Freedom Day

Alexandre-Gabriel Descamps, *Françoise Liberté*

Don't forget the context of what we have to compete with. The all-pervasive (social) media messages that we are bombarded with, the environment in which we have to work. We don't just need the right way to get through to people, we also need to be present in people's lives regularly and dependably if we are to break through the information overload that the right uses to create their racist hegemony.

Right-wing counterculture

If we appear to be supporting the status quo and the far right appears to be challenging it, even when in reality it's the other way round, it begs the question: how did we get here? During lockdown, the left in general was promoting common sense healthcare advice that we should wear masks, socially distance, stay at home to protect each other. We made masks to share, we set up mutual aid programmes to help others. Although coming from a position of class solidarity, this position directly (although unintentionally) aligned us with what the state was saying. But for many working class people staying at home just wasn't an option, they had to go to work. In contrast, the

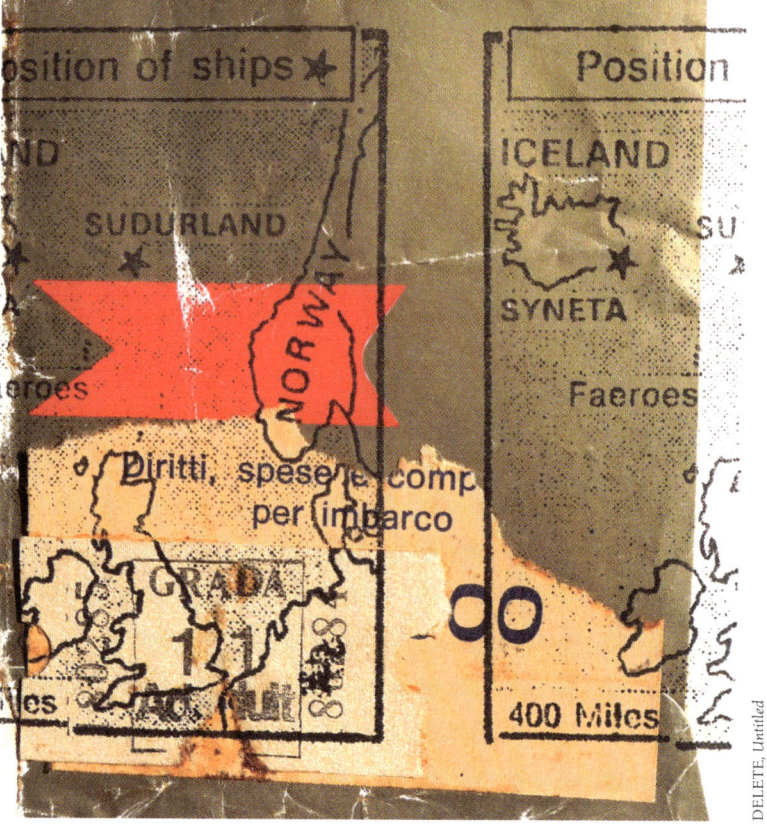

DELETE, Untitled

right's attitude was all about individual freedom, and fuck everyone else. Fuck the state and its rules, let us work. A growing number of left-leaning people, resorting to conspiracy fantasies to explain an unstable and uncertain world, were very quickly pulled into their orbit, not ours. Once again, what the right was saying reinforced their ideas and gradually led many into their movement without them even realising it.

Fast forward to today and the people who are attacking the cops, burning police cars and demanding change are being led by the far right. In response, anti-fascists are being seen as the ones organising unity demonstrations, supporting the status quo and being praised by the police. When this happens, we have a fundamental problem. We are no longer the revolutionaries, the right are. Because they were carrying out unmediated activity. They were not calling on the new Labour government to change anything, they were trying to do it directly themselves. They were attempting their ethnic cleansing in the context of opposition to the 'elite'. It's not their demands so much as how they are aiming to achieve them, that is seen as revolutionary. And to an extent that is what is driving the participation of (some) angry young working class men. Although our unity demonstrations were also a form of direct action in which we organised a tremendous show of force to reclaim our streets against the fascists, we were at the same time perceived as passively standing squarely with the current state of society (and its representatives in blue) to protect it from the previous week's rioters. As if they were aberrations, and we wanted to go back to normal.

Now, responding to their pogroms with demonstrations of love and unity doesn't change the material conditions that make others angry. It may allow us to go home feeling like the far right have been faced down, but obviously the circumstances that created their explosion of rage are still present. We have been able to push that moment into the future, but it's still coming. And we need to be better prepared for it next time.

Perhaps we would get more traction with messages and action of revenge/resentment against the actual class structures that make our lives shit, rather than persisting with the Guardian reader 'love thy neighbour' approach, which ignores the pain and genuine, but misdirected, rage being felt. Perhaps we need to demonstrate that we feel that rage against the status quo too, but that our anger is against those who would divide us against ourselves so they can lord it over us.

DELETE, Untitled

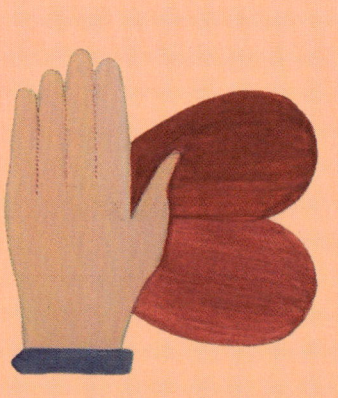

Our counterculture of care

'Hope and grief can coexist, and if we wish to transform the world, we must learn to hold and to process both simultaneously. That process will, as ever, involve reaching for community.'

Kelly Hayes and Mariame Kaba,
'Let This Radicalize You'

If people hate the system as much as we do, but simply don't believe there's a possibility of changing it, how can we win? The only future that the far right holds out to us is one where we are in the gutter fighting for crumbs with other desperate people. Our lives are represented to us as a zero-sum game (I win, you lose) where we're all in competition with each other for limited resources, whether social and physical—like money, housing and healthcare—or symbolic resources—like value, clout and respect.

The far right's 'Save Our Kids' slogan becomes a tragedy when you realise what their politics actually have in store for all of our children in a climate-ravaged world. Maybe highlighting the path to that doomsday scenario will help us drive a wedge between the right and their support base. That is our essential task. But to begin that process, we have to offer the prospect of meaningful change towards something better. Something people actually want. Change that offers concrete choices, which mean something in the context in which we live. Not just words but actions. What that change is, what gets changed, what replaces it, is less important than the demonstration that it is actually possible for us to do it at all.

As powerful as our rage is against capital, we also have a new world growing in our hearts. We need to offer people a positive choice for the future as well as being ferocious in our opposition to the way we have to live today.

One encouraging thing about the ONS survey mentioned at the start of this article was that even in this dog-eat-dog world, 70% of respondents reported that in general, they trust most people. All across the planet, when disasters and emergencies strike, we get glimpses of a different way of human interaction which allows mutual aid and care for each other to bloom from some part of ourselves that has been hidden away while we battle through daily life under capitalism.

As argued in 'Haunted by the Ghost...' the work to rebuild the collective subject is a fundamental part of this. We need to build a real alternative that works, and to rebuild the belief that we can change everything, that we're not in a doom loop. We can escape. We can combine an organisational effort with the lessons we have learned about how to get our ideas across and fight for the future.

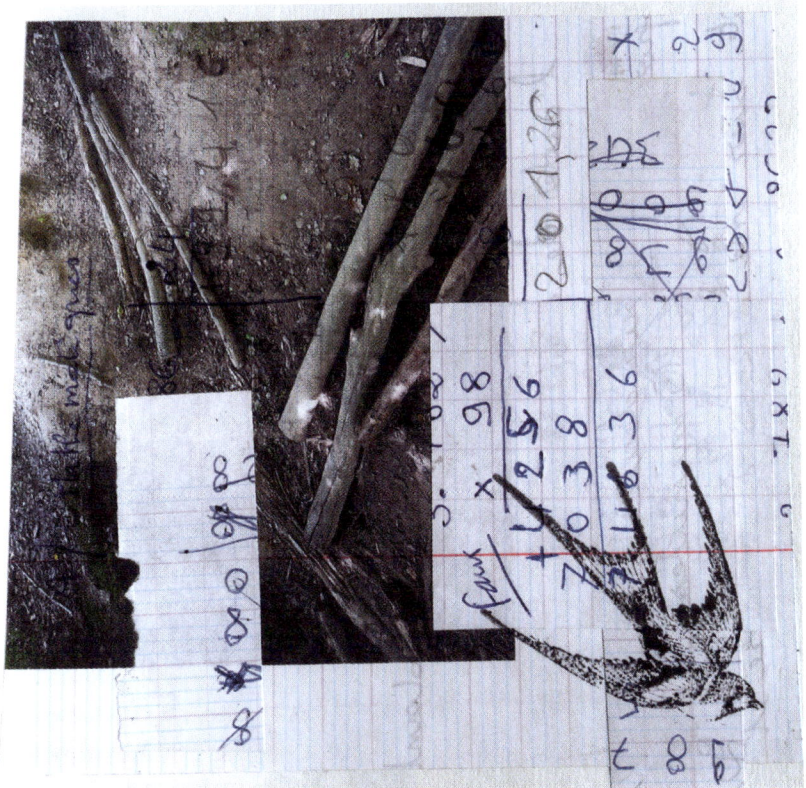

DELETE, Untitled

Stick It To The Man

Razorsmile

It's easy to get lost amongst the images of capitalism. Particularly in the city.

One of the joys of being outside the city is that the cacophony of adverts is replaced by the silence of grass. But the revolution needs the city. The revolution breathes on the streets of urban spaces, in a land of the mass human—mass workers, mass consumers, mass transit, mass housing. Capitalist power is always restless when facing a mass, aware of its fragility in a horizon of riots and rampage. It uses its images to organise our dreams, to domesticate our desires and keep us captured in its own world.

How can we refuse the imagery of capitalism in the city? How can we work for the revolution against capital and its imagery? It's easy to think that working for the revolution is complicated. Often we hear about sacrifice, discipline, dedication. If I wanted those things I'd join a church.

Revolution is messiness. Dirty talk. Refusal of the lines others draw. Reclaiming the streets—and the images of the streets.

All photos by Razorsmile

Refusal cannot begin until it is more than a thought. Refusal is given form in an act, however small, but we have to find a way to refuse without destroying or harming ourselves. And we have to find a starting point for our acts.

Like most things, it's often good to begin small. Things can escalate quickly, so gain experience where you can and don't be afraid of the small act. It can open doors and windows and let a gust of hope breeze in. Each small act is part of building a new earth.

Order some stickers from a website. Pick some up from a social centre, or from a street stall in town. Put them in your pocket. Go for a walk and begin to look around. Let your eyes pay attention to the gallery of the street. Pay attention to the new and the old, the shiny colours of the fresh and the faded ages of the past.

Don't follow your usual routes. Take a detour. You cannot see what you don't look for, so look for the gallery of the streets. When you do this you will begin to see the vibrant conversation of the masses, of us. We speak in the cracks, marking the lamp posts and street furniture with our dreams, slogans, images. You will encounter here the other side of the media, the main street media.

Here in the gallery of the streets are the secret societies of tags, the images of the dreamers and the slogans and calls of the revolution. Here you begin to realise that the constant flow of the images of capitalism cannot resist our creativity. Capitalism cannot keep the streets clean, and that is evidence of our strength.

This is a vital lesson. The secret of the revolution is that we are irresistible. We cannot be cleaned up or cleaned out. Try as hard as it can, capitalism is always running after us, trying to capture our creativity and life. It wants us to believe its dream of the world. It wants to persuade us that these adverts are a normal everyday truth rather than the bizarre monstrosities they really are.

Capitalism's successes are everywhere, but so are its failures. If we only listen to the privileged voices of the news and media and politicos and cowards, we can be caught inside the dream of the so-called 'real world'. But take a moment, pay attention and notice the revolution everywhere. Resistance flows like water through the cracks in the dam.

On the streets, at the crossings and on the signs, we see each other as we disobey and refuse the clean lines of the world organised and dreamed of by capitalism. The fascist heart of capital cannot stand disorganisation, mess, dirt, the mixtures of colours and sounds that make life vibrant. The first act of the fist of revolution can be the simple one of joining the secret society, sticking it to the man, sticking it to the world around.

As you walk the streets with your stickers, covering over the fascists, dirtying up the capitalist world and marking your movements through the city, you join a society of friends. You take a first step into the world of the revolution. Don't stop there. Take another step. Then another. Before you know it you will be amongst friends, working for the revolution, believing in a new earth that is already on the streets, rising.

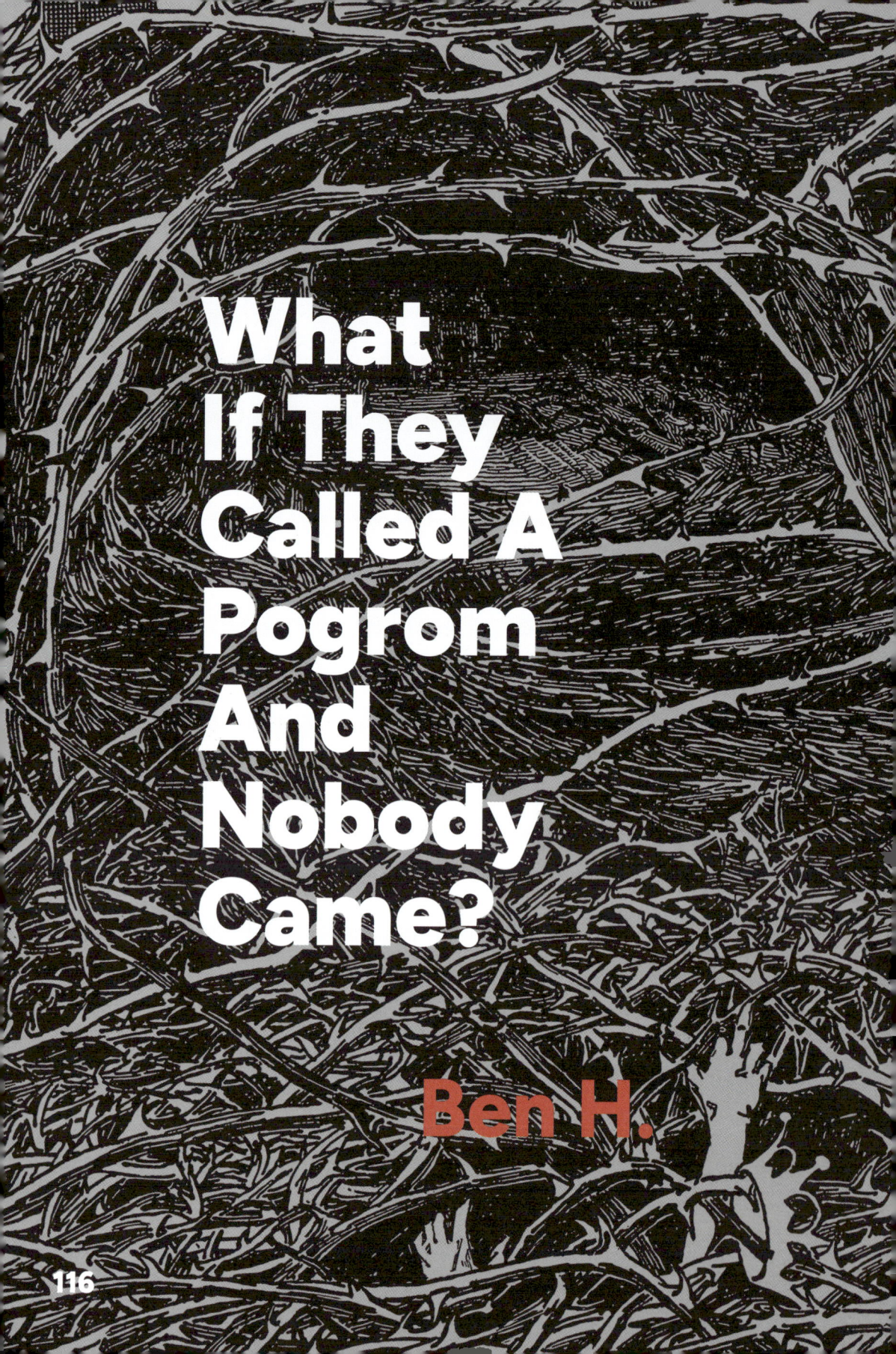

What If They Called A Pogrom And Nobody Came?

Ben H.

Wilhelm Jordan, *Sharp Thorns*

On the 29th July 2024, a British boy murdered three young girls in an indiscriminate attack in Southport, Merseyside. The law normally prohibits reporting the details of underage offenders. Exploiting this vacuum, within hours the far-right dissident media had already filled it with self-serving fabrications: an Arabic-sounding name, a 'small boats' migration origin story and assumed links to Islamic fundamentalism.

The attack triggered a wave of reaction that had already been primed by a media landscape of Islamophobia and fear of migration. The outgoing Conservative cabinet's apparent racial and ethnic diversity was either purely superficial, or perhaps actually provided ideological cover for their increasingly cruel nativist politics over the past few years.

Two major reasons help to explain this. Outside of the party, they were pandering to a vocal subset of their supporters who they feared would vote for the far-right Reform party and extinguish the Conservatives' chances of returning to government for a generation. Internally, leading Tory figures ended up competing with each other to win the most hardline reputation, thereby strengthening their chances in the future competition to become leader of the opposition. Whilst the incoming Labour government scrapped some of the more ludicrous policies such as the Rwanda deportation plan, under the bonnet the racist and anti-immigration machine continued to operate normally.

In its mostly online spaces, the grassroots right had also worked itself up into a lather. In their grotesque imaginary, an inverted D-Day was already taking place, with countless 'fighting-age men' arriving in small boats at Kent. They also put forward the narrative of a two-tier legal system, under which white British people were unfairly persecuted whilst Black people and Asians were coddled. Finally, they claimed that lawful society was under violent attack from environmental and anticolonial/antiracist protesters.

On the night after the murders, 30th July, a mosque in Southport was attacked, injuring more than fifty police officers. As the left knows from experience, Britain's urban police forces are usually a dab hand at turning political unrest and public disorder into paralysing stalemates; not for us the burning barricades, melee combat or tear gas clouds often seen elsewhere in Europe. But on that night in Southport and elsewhere in the days that followed, the police were outnumbered and cowed by the willingness for direct confrontation. Following the name of one of the popular Telegram channels, it wouldn't be an exaggeration to dub this wave of unrest the 'Southport Uprising'.

DELETE, *Untitled*

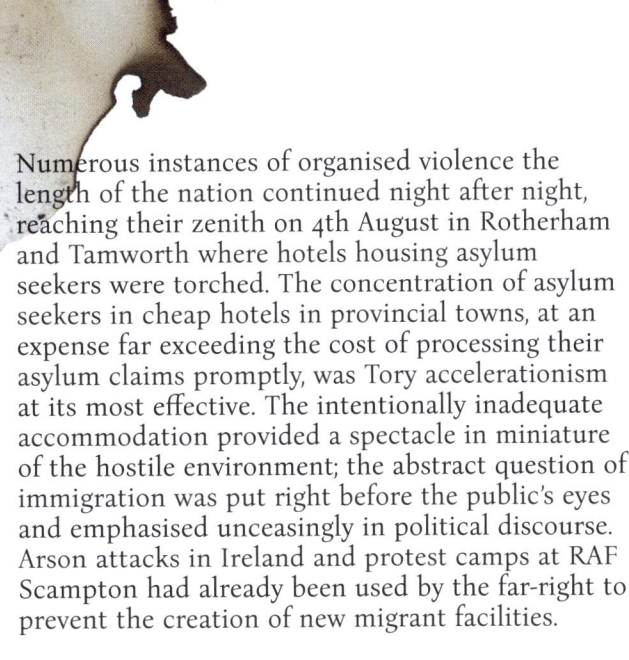

Numerous instances of organised violence the length of the nation continued night after night, reaching their zenith on 4th August in Rotherham and Tamworth where hotels housing asylum seekers were torched. The concentration of asylum seekers in cheap hotels in provincial towns, at an expense far exceeding the cost of processing their asylum claims promptly, was Tory accelerationism at its most effective. The intentionally inadequate accommodation provided a spectacle in miniature of the hostile environment; the abstract question of immigration was put right before the public's eyes and emphasised unceasingly in political discourse. Arson attacks in Ireland and protest camps at RAF Scampton had already been used by the far-right to prevent the creation of new migrant facilities.

At this point, the disorder passed beyond the diffuse violence of the riot and assumed the deadly precision of the pogrom. We should clearly differentiate a pogrom from a riot, a lynching or an uprising: it is a unilateral, collective punishment of a minority by the majority, motivated by the belief that the state will not otherwise directly enforce the majority demands, and executed without high levels of preplanned organisation. In reality, and despite claims to the contrary, explicit support from the authorities is not a defining feature of historical pogroms, but we can certainly conclude that pogromists are, at least, influenced by the racist tendencies of the state and society, and act with the hope of impunity.

In contrast with the 'nick 'em quick' dogma proposed by police chiefs, and the accelerated justice procedures promised by the government, the expectation of soft treatment was not entirely in vain. In Rotherham, just six were arrested, and in Tamworth none, when the respective asylum hotels in these towns were torched. Many more would be arrested at larger metropolitan demonstrations, or later at home on the basis of recorded evidence. Nevertheless only around seven hundred arrests had been booked by the end of the second week after the riots.

This contrasts with the 2011 riots in London, largely carried out by working class young men radicalised by the police killing of Mark Duggan. Faced with a reaction against the State's violent powers, the courts ran round the clock to prosecute four thousand arrestees, and nearly eight hundred and fifty were in prison by the following month.

This is not to claim that the state supported the pogroms of August 2024. In truth, the forces of order simply were overwhelmed in some specific locations. More broadly, their long-term focus on Islamism, the environmentalist movement and left activism had led them to underestimate the far-right threat. The government has little to offer apart from symbolic action such as exemplary punishments, firm words against the attackers, retrospective praise of liberal antiracism, and suggestions to proscribe the English Defence League, an organisation defunct since 2016 (if not earlier).

Pogroms are most often associated with the history of antisemitic violence in Europe and elsewhere. They have rarely occurred in Britain, but it would be misleading to say that they are unprecedented. Immediately after the First World War, there was violent unrest in several British dock towns such as Glasgow, Cardiff and Liverpool. The post-war depression had reduced employment, and there was stiff competition for jobs and housing between white residents, recently-demobilised soldiers from the West Indies, and West African sailors.

The British Seafarers Union and National Sailors' and Fireman's Union promoted the narrative that non-whites were undercutting white wages, and there was widespread eugenicist anxiety at intermarriages made evident by census records.

A physical confrontation began in Glasgow when sailors gathered to sign contracts *en masse*. White aggression quickly intensified, culminating several months later with crowds of up to 10,000 in Liverpool attacking Black people and vandalising their homes and businesses. The state's response was to arrest Black combatants disproportionately, detain hundreds of residents 'for their own safety', and make plans for them to be put in concentration camps or deported. The violence was generally against Black and Arab residents, but led to refusal to employ Chinese and Irish workers as well. Although not actively condoned by the state, as few pogroms are, we can easily see the influence of nativist labour politics behind the unrest. By the 1920s, thousands of ethnic minority workers had been laid off or 'repatriated'. In that

Félix Vallotton, *The Demonstration*

DELETE, *Untitled*

sense, the punishment/extermination goal of the pogroms had been achieved by subsequent actions taken by the state.

In 1919, as in 2024, no amount of racist organising could have directly brought about the pogroms. Nevertheless, pogroms only occur when conditions make it easier for them to occur than not. The racism of far-right agitators and a racist government driven by the rhetoric of nativist politics create ideal conditions for a pogrom to explode as soon as some trigger event occurs.

We may yet see that the government in 2025 also gives way to pogromist demands in order to restore a social peace. In fact, in late August 2024 the Home Office promised a 'large surge' in deportations; a hundred more National Crime Agency intelligence officers targeting people smugglers; massive fines and forcible closure orders for businesses employing irregular immigrants; the reopening of two 'removal centres'; and new fast-track deportation agreements with several countries.

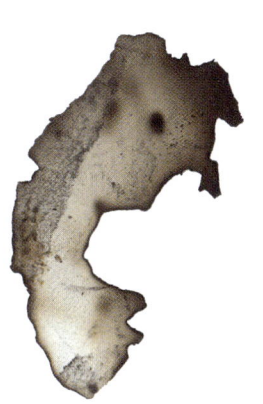

Despite this historical precedent, both state and antifascist forces have nevertheless been forced to reckon with a genuine development in the nature of fascist organisation. A tendency towards disintegration has pulled apart the old forms of fascist organising in recent years: the traditional far-right electoral parties like the British National Party have mostly lost their supporters to the more polite populist nativism of Reform and the Conservatives; street movements have been replaced by individual influencers and video streamers; even fascist elements within the police and armed forces have been disrupted by (shallow, but genuine) institutional liberalisation. In their place a genuinely horizontal and spontaneous way of organising has evolved, albeit one grounded entirely in the virtual domain. For the first time, we have seen the national arson target list emerge as a tool of terror. This was the list of a few dozen targets widely circulated in Telegram chats like 'Southport Rise Up' and 'Southport Awake', mostly consisting of refugee advice centres and legal firms. Online fascists also repeatedly shared an accompanying guide to arson developed by the Russian/Ukrainian 'National Socialism/White Power Crew'.

The notion of 'stochastic terrorism' refers to the idea that 'random' acts of violence will emerge spontaneously when certain people are influenced by an inflammatory culture or media landscape. Those who incite the violence are isolated from those who actually carry out the attacks. Often they are influential people using dog-whistles, which is to say coded or imprecise language intended to be understood by only an extreme subset of the audience, while maintaining a certain deniability. The chain of causation between influencer and perpetrator is usually disrupted by media narratives that focus on the attacker's mental state, or that portray them as self-radicalising lone wolves. But as in the case of Thomas Mair, who murdered Jo Cox MP, violent crimes are more likely to occur when an individual is bombarded consistently with violent, politicised content that adds to an already existing mainstream media diet of Islamophobia and anti-migrant sentiment.

It doesn't quite make sense to say that fascist organisations are 'doing' stochastic fascism, that there is some kind of strategy beneath the list of targets. The idea that fascists put out certain callouts as 'decoys' to draw antifascists to certain locations while they really plan to target others also seems unrealistic in practice. Rather, this new form of fascism must be seen as something enabled by current material conditions and methods of communication.

Where organisations do act within these new communication platforms, they are generally riding the coattails of a spontaneous movement, trying to bootstrap disorder up to the level of political struggle. The association of known fascist organisers with the disorder is purely opportunistic; they have been taken by surprise just as political organisers of all affiliations are typically overtaken by events. In Sunderland, neo-Nazis who were in the area for a Blood and Honour gig joined in the disorder, and Patriotic Alternative tried to build on the disorder by promoting their 'Free Sam Melia' demonstration at HMP Hull. Activists were seen at local attacks wearing t-shirts with that slogan, but turnout at the event was, as usual, limited to their sad rump of engaged activists. It's unlikely that even one attacker out of a hundred knows who Sam Melia is.

DELETE, Untitled

One far-right niche that has been undeniably close to the centre of things is the new breed of fascist livestreamers, which include the likes of Aaron Johnson (himself previously convicted for football-related offences). Johnson was convicted of inciting racial hatred after live streaming himself threatening asylum seekers inside a hotel in Stockport. These streamers have become significant media influences over the past few years, positioning themselves as conspiratorial 'auditors' of police and others, freelance journalists or even independent border security agents. Almost by definition their activities are individual, eccentric and opposed to large-scale organisation, but nonetheless they are an important part of the online far-right media ecosystem. The nature of social media platforms means that they are able to reach numbers that would be unimaginable for traditional fascist organisations.

In other online spheres, the recent success of London protests organised by Stephen Yaxley-Lennon (AKA Tommy Robinson) has also reinvigorated football hooligan groups, mostly on Facebook. Known organisers from the Democratic Football Lads' Alliance have been drawing people out of the insecure Facebook groups into more private regional Whatsapp chats, agitating for violent action. But like other far-right organisations, it is clear that they are tailing the wave of spontaneous violence rather than playing any leadership role. Their insecure communication and fractious, leak-prone membership could lead to disproportionate numbers of convictions for known hooligans. In fact, the Metropolitan Police commissioner claimed that 70% of those convicted in the days following the disorder had previous violent convictions, and 'some' had football banning orders. But this shouldn't deceive us into thinking that they constituted a vanguard. Rather, they were just more likely to be caught and convicted: many had filmed themselves during the action, providing low-hanging fruit for the police operation.

Meanwhile, the mainstream media's search for culpable actors has predictably led back to two of their reliable bogeymen: firstly Yaxley-Lennon, his profile being high in that moment due to his large demonstration in London the week before the events. Although he initially circulated the false claims about the identity of the murderer, he has otherwise had little to do with the unrest apart from existing within the same football lad culture milieu. Secondly, the liberal spectre of 'Russian online disinformation' was blamed, a tactic which conveniently assuages the media class' guilt at their complicity in anti-immigrant sentiment, while promoting their condescending assumption that white working class people are so stupid that they really will believe anything a bot says on Twitter.

Félix Vallotton, *Paris Crowd*

In truth, there is no sign of a unified plan behind the fascist arson lists. Antifascists are used to the idea of 'chasing ghosts', ie. getting distracted from the reality in front of us by rumours of fascists elsewhere; but usually these rumours are generated by people on our side. Now, online fascists were collating and circulating rumours of their own from various, unspecified sources; hoping, no doubt, to improve the odds by publicising them, but probably not expecting them all to turn into something real (nor creating throwaway targets as decoys). This is something qualitatively different to the familiar overambitious plan or botched callout.

As far as we know, none of the legal firms or migrant support offices listed in the frequently-circulated 'arson list' were seriously attacked, although the presence of known local Nazi organisers in places such as Birmingham dispel the notion that they were empty threats in order to spread defenders more thinly. Where serious attacks took place, they were invariably against hotels housing asylum seekers first, and mosques a distant second. The list consisted of publicly

Félix Vallotton, *The Department Store*

available addresses, with errors that suggested online research rather than local knowledge. For instance, a residential address in Nottingham was ascribed to a law firm as it was the registered office of a self-employed lawyer. The list had the wonky alphabetisation of a document being carelessly compiled, to which was added a few confidently-claimed, plausible errors characteristic of a ChatGPT response.

The political act is the creation of the list of targets. The actual execution is carried out by those who are spontaneously moved to action. In a way, this predictably reflects the diffuse nature of Telegram organising. Chat groups come and go, the social capital of known organisers is defused by anonymity, and influence is measured in terms of online engagement rather than real-world feet on the ground. Where any demonstration has been ascribed to a particular name or brand, these are overwhelmingly vapid slogans revealing the opportunism and acquisitiveness of memetic ideology in the 2020s: 'Stop the Boats'; 'Enough is Enough'; 'Save our Children'.

The shock of its novelty should not blind us to the ineffectiveness of this new strategy. August 7th, the planned night of fire, was marked by large antiracist mobilisations and extremely low fascist turnout. In several places fascist gatherings were outnumbered more than a hundred to one. Even in the places where the forces were more balanced, no successful arson attacks took place. The fascist callouts reflected the kinds of power fantasy politics which thrive in online spaces where the most extreme voices are concentrated, amplified and echoed. An analysis of the largest Southport-related chats found that although they had tens of thousands of members at their peak, fewer than three hundred people had engaged regularly with them. No doubt, their membership was vastly inflated by rubberneckers, stay-at-homes, and antifascist observers.

Nevertheless there was some consolation here for the fascists. In the online rumour mill, the presence of a target on the list was often regarded as a genuine threat, regardless of whether there was any real indication that people would turn up. With recent experience of the early hotel burnings still in mind, this led to a certain overreaction that intensified, rather than relieved, anxiety for the most affected communities. Businesses were closed for the day, in places even boarded up, in anticipation of an attack that never came.

Perhaps it's no surprise that saboteurs and pogromists, for the most part, don't announce their targets in advance. In fact, effective sabotage can be done against overwhelming force, provided that the saboteurs have the element of surprise. On the 6th August, a mere six Palestine Action members were able to break through the secure perimeter of an Elbit research and manufacturing facility, destroying materials intended for the genocide in Palestine. In contrast, the fascist target list exposes

DELETE, Untitled

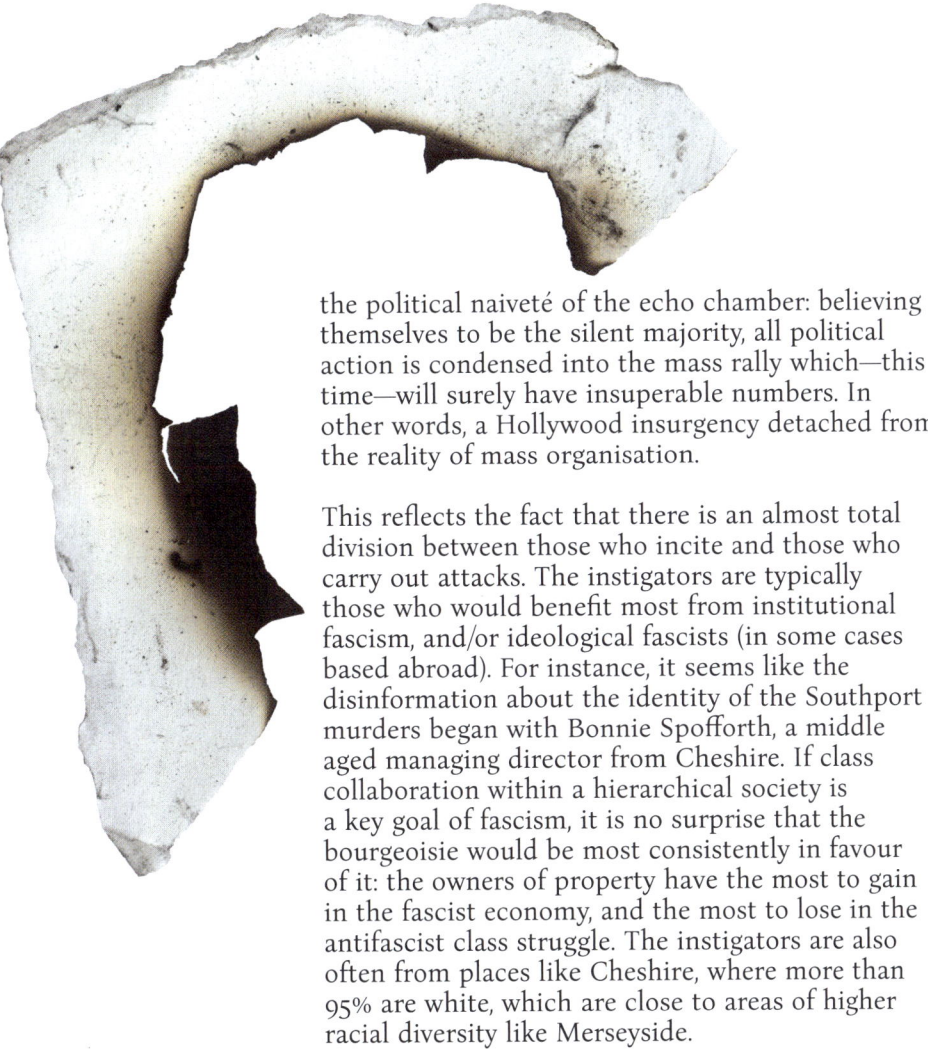

the political naiveté of the echo chamber: believing themselves to be the silent majority, all political action is condensed into the mass rally which—this time—will surely have insuperable numbers. In other words, a Hollywood insurgency detached from the reality of mass organisation.

This reflects the fact that there is an almost total division between those who incite and those who carry out attacks. The instigators are typically those who would benefit most from institutional fascism, and/or ideological fascists (in some cases based abroad). For instance, it seems like the disinformation about the identity of the Southport murders began with Bonnie Spofforth, a middle aged managing director from Cheshire. If class collaboration within a hierarchical society is a key goal of fascism, it is no surprise that the bourgeoisie would be most consistently in favour of it: the owners of property have the most to gain in the fascist economy, and the most to lose in the antifascist class struggle. The instigators are also often from places like Cheshire, where more than 95% are white, which are close to areas of higher racial diversity like Merseyside.

In many cases, their involvement reflects racial anxieties and fantasies rather than political fascism per se, but online far-right spaces are often international in character, featuring ideological fascists from different parts of the world. For instance, research by Red Flare linked the widespread arson guides to a neo-Nazi actually living in Finland.

Modern online spaces also create opportunities for right-wing influences to profit from provocative statements made from afar. Wayne O'Rourke was jailed for his X posts inciting violence in Southport, a hundred and fifty miles away from his home in Lincoln. The engagement with his ninety thousand followers, and millions others exposed via the timeline algorithm, brought him over £1,400 a month under Musk's revenue-sharing system. Grifters have always been able to make money from the far-right scene (either from sales or donations), but only recently have social media platforms made it profitable for relatively casual users to seek out more inflammatory and emotive content.

In contrast, the actual foot soldiers are naturally much more likely to be associated with the local area. Their economic and cultural positioning make them particularly receptive to violent rhetoric and, of course, more likely to get expedited judgments and harsh sentences. Masses of working class people were not becoming fascists overnight, but fascism provided the spark that lit a pre-existing powder keg. The reporting of this distorts the perception of the class basis of fascism by focussing on its foot soldiers rather than its leadership.

This raises a recurring problem for antifascism. We are often only able to intervene directly in confrontation with 'street fascists'. While never forgetting the actual role that militant antifascism can play in stopping racist violence, nor the need to

expose, confront and hold accountable those who actually carry out the violence, the broader political context is that these people are victims of structural oppression themselves. Without neglecting our bread-and-butter tactics, we also need to find ways to strike directly at the powerful who deflect their own culpability onto immigrants and non-whites.

What will the far-right have gained from their experience of these pivotal ten days? Both positive and negative assessments could be made about the balance of forces: in places, the control function of the state was challenged, while antifascists and local racialised communities were, for a time, on the back foot.

On the other hand, the violence did not live up to the fascist power fantasies: the number of pogromists was small, compared to other similarly intense outbreaks of disorder; the media and public opinion largely closed ranks against the anti-immigration and anti-Islam protesters who the

Félix Vallotton, *The Shower*

week before had been broadly within mainstream discourse. But the experience of a moment of struggle that goes beyond the hypothetical, even if unsuccessful, can be a powerful motivator for future militancy (as those of us on the left know equally well).

The state's response will also have fuelled the sense of injustice that underlies the latest fascist talking point, so-called 'two-tier policing'. The reversal of victim and offender is a key feature of fascist propaganda, and the notion that white people are being particularly oppressed by the British police is especially laughable. Nevertheless, the law-and-order positioning of a new government trying to forcibly keep the lid on contagious disorder plays into this illusion. The Prime Minister, Keir Starmer, was Director of Public Prosecutions (the third most senior prosecutor in England and Wales) during the 2011 riots after the police killing of Mark Duggan. The government response in 2024 naturally continued along similar lines, aiming to achieve incarceration within mere days of the offence.

Attempting to defuse the online element, the state aggressively went after those whose 'malicious communications' had contributed to the unrest. Social media platforms are designed to amplify and spread content which is provocative, giving excessive real-world influence to statements which in normal contexts would be considered outrageous or simply stupid. Whether the punishment ought to reflect an action's consequences or its intention is up for debate, but the incarceration of people for bigoted statements targeted at their personal circles will only increase the right-wing sense of grievance.

DELETE, Untitled

Likewise the prosecution of children as young as eleven for violent disorder, and even a fifteen year-old for riot, the most serious public order offence, is likely to aggravate rather than calm the swell of anger and prejudice. This calculating cruelty of the state, its single-minded reliance on carceral solutions, comes as no surprise to many Black and Asian boys and young men, nor to many poor and working class people in general, but it is a particularly offensive shock to a reactionary white culture, which sees its race as deserving to be above the law, to find itself vindictively targeted by it. While we would disagree with them on almost everything else, we can't deny that this is a terrible and harmful thing to do to children.

For the ideologues on the far-right, the backlash must have created an impression: the state, identified with the new Labour government, supposedly dishing out particularly vindictive repression from above; a culturally alien, metropolitan and multicultural antiracist opposition on the streets; and a small field of their fascist allies caught between them both.

In other words, this is a variant of the 'three way fight' identified by militant antifascists. From the far-right perspective, this raises technical and ideological challenges long considered on the militant left: retreat and strengthen within existing bases of power, find ways to organise across unhelpful divides... and what to do about the state?

In the first case, retrenchments on the right may be similar to those on the left: organisations of political reproduction and mutual aid, social spaces with an explicitly political character, siloes and echo-chambers of increasing homogeneity.

In the second case, where we on the left wish to disrupt racial division by organising along class lines, fascists will aim for cross-class alliances and the conditional aid for poor white people practised by Patriotic Alternative and Homeland.

In the third case, where we may see the final end of fascism in the total destruction of the state as we know it, fascists are more likely to think in terms of realigning state power with their interests. This could be by parliamentary change that gives them ideological cover, a revolutionary rupture that does away with the liberalised nation-state in favour of a race-state; or (in some parts of the world) by withdrawal, survivalist autarky or secession.

Antifascism has to periodically reinvent itself; in practice usually a reactive process triggered by innovations on the right. The work of the coming weeks and months will be to continue to assess the developments, create new formations and innovate new tactics, with analysis at the service of our goals rather than taking a primary position. There was some predictable and justified criticism of the

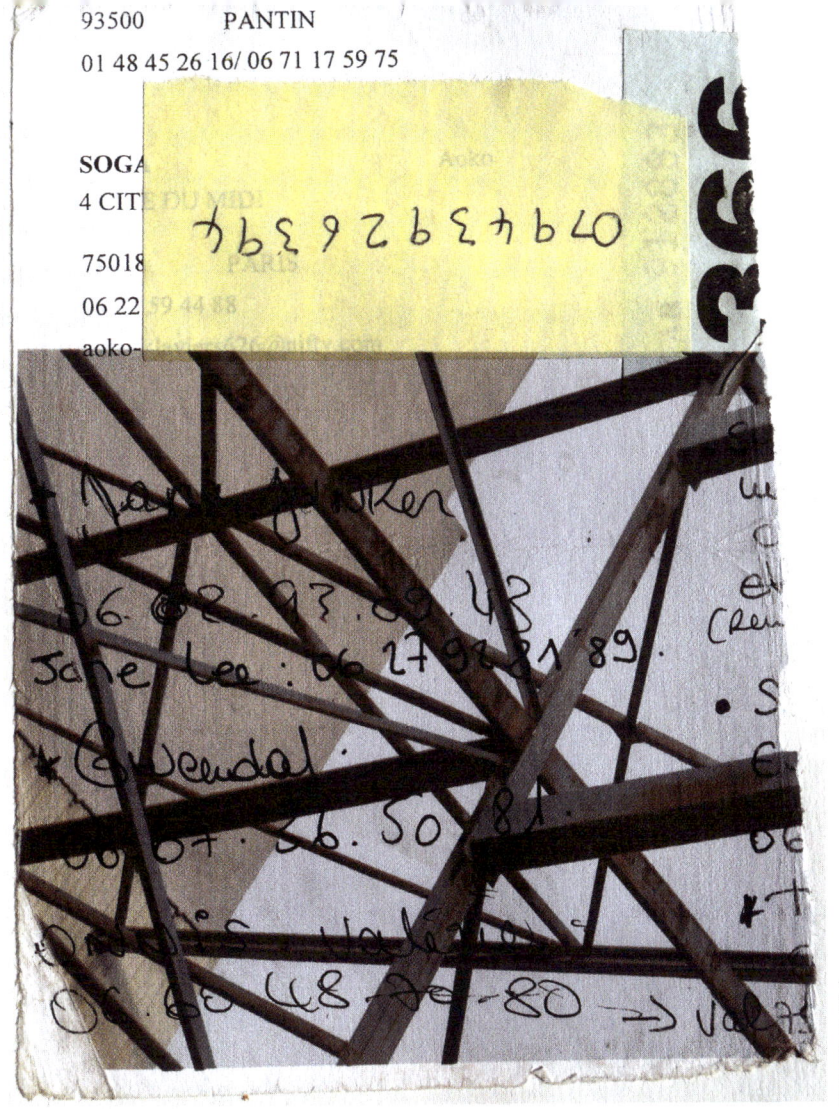

DELETE, Untitled

excessive focus on some areas above others, which naturally favoured cosmopolitan multiracial urban areas to the detriment of provincial towns where violence was more likely. The reality of antifascist organisation in these frantic ten days was that it wasn't possible to make a considered assessment of the threat. Now we are a bit better informed, and can see more clearly.

Firstly, there should be no action without strategy. Previous antifascist crises, such as the much-analysed 'A22 PDX' situation[1], have illustrated that a knee-jerk application of the principle, 'we go where they go', can lead to half-baked and dangerous plans

1. 22nd 2021 Proud Boys disorder in Portland, Oregon—see https://threewayfight.org/understanding-a22-pdx-discussion-and-analysis-for-the-antifascist-movements/

Félix Vallotton, *The Anarchist*

which cause more damage than doing nothing. This is not to say that we should decide in advance to cede particular territory to the fascists, but rather that our capabilities are finite and some risks have to be accepted rather than mitigated.

For instance, hundreds of local people assembled without much external organisation in the Bordesley Green area of Birmingham on the 5th August. A majority Asian, working class community with a history of resistance to fascist and state violence, Bordesley Green would have been an inappropriate and unnecessary location for externally-based antifascist groups to have a callout. A small group of fascists streamed themselves driving past the massive crowd, and understandably decided to call off their demo.

For different reasons, affluent city centres are also not in much need of a mass antifascist rally. We can probably assume that any attempts at violence will be handled by police and private security whose main interest is the protection of private property.

A better focus for antifascist resistance is the large provincial town or small city, the localised pockets of economic decline and racial tensions. Local people are receptive to the simple explanations of online fascists; they may be able to see before their eyes a significant number of migrants where previously there were none, thanks to the absurd asylum hotel system. Racialised communities are smaller, less self-organised and more vulnerable than in larger urban areas.

The antifascist mobilisation should be only one part of local left-wing organising in these areas, alongside militant responses to state violence, the housing crisis and workplace exploitation. While direct confrontation of fascists is always going to be a keystone of antifascist mobilisations, away from the front line our demonstrations should be a festival of resistance, with social and political reproduction at their core—this means not speeches and placards, but music, food, discussions and entertainment for all ages.

In general, we should be wary of the tendency of 'chasing ghosts'. We should always be asking, is this threat credible, can we identify a clear enemy, can we determine a meaningful goal for our actions on the day?

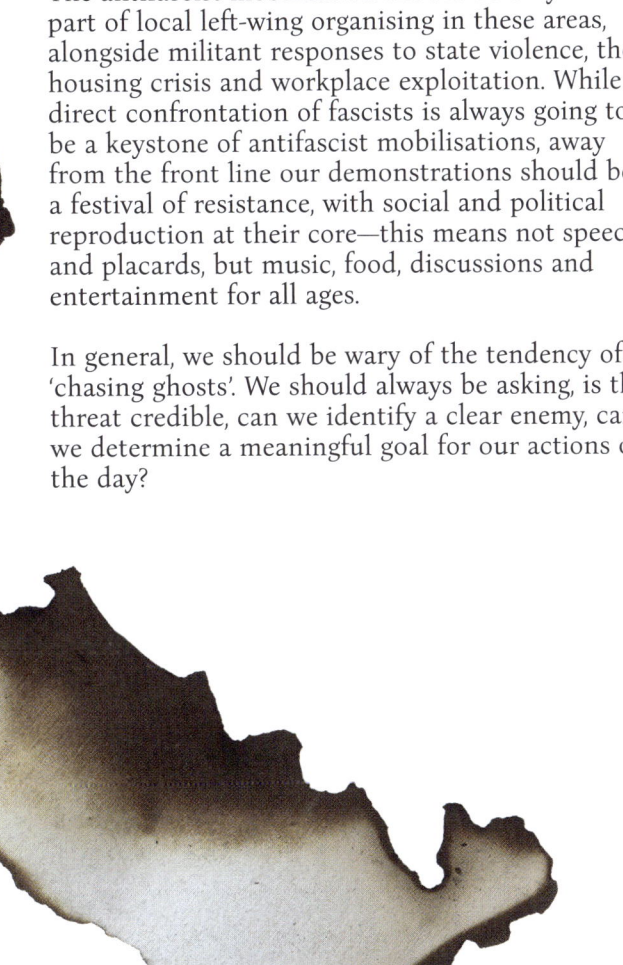

Finally, although it may seem depressing, we must not overlook the strategic needs to have a realistic rather than idealistic assessment of our own forces, and never willingly seek out a losing battle. If this runs against the grain of the saviour/sacrificial ethic at the heart of some antifascist thought, then good.

Fascism has changed abruptly, and we need to too. We are not currently in a place where we can act strategically as proposed above. There are many reasons for this, which are being rehashed in antifascist group discussions around the country. To pick just one, our circles of intelligence-gathering had been slow to adapt to the new, fractured nature of online fascism, which is now not just an extreme fringe but absolutely central to real-world fascist activity in a way that it has never been before.

In the run-up to the 7th August, the proposed night of arson, the best we could do was to make decisions based on negative inference—if a callout didn't seem to be getting any traction online, then perhaps we could assume that it wasn't likely to go off. The danger of this was obvious—without deep embedment in heterogeneous fascist online spaces, it was impossible to say whether a callout really was just hot air, or if we were just listening in on the wrong people. This level of embedment is hard, horrible work; it takes a certain type of comrade to develop the online persona and relationships to get the intel, and a whole structure of other comrades who are able to support them, process and make good use of the information gathered. Within our networks of resistance, existing or new, we should attempt to both spread the labour and avoid reduplicating efforts.

This strategic outlook can't exist if local groups are working in isolation, or if they are focussed solely on specific forms of right-wing organisation rather than the broader context. Our organisation needs to reflect the fact that antifascism is just one facet of a broader social struggle. Fascism is more eclectic and disjointed than ever, but it is also sustained by its roots in a fertile political and economic culture. Our side will be characterised by its diversity as well, but every element of it needs to put down stronger roots within oppressed communities. The goal is to simultaneously displace fascism's allure for the marginalised communities it appeals to, while always building the integral capacity to resist it in the marginalised communities it menaces. 🌺

DELETE, Untitled

Three Notes on Thinking as an Organisation

Enda O.

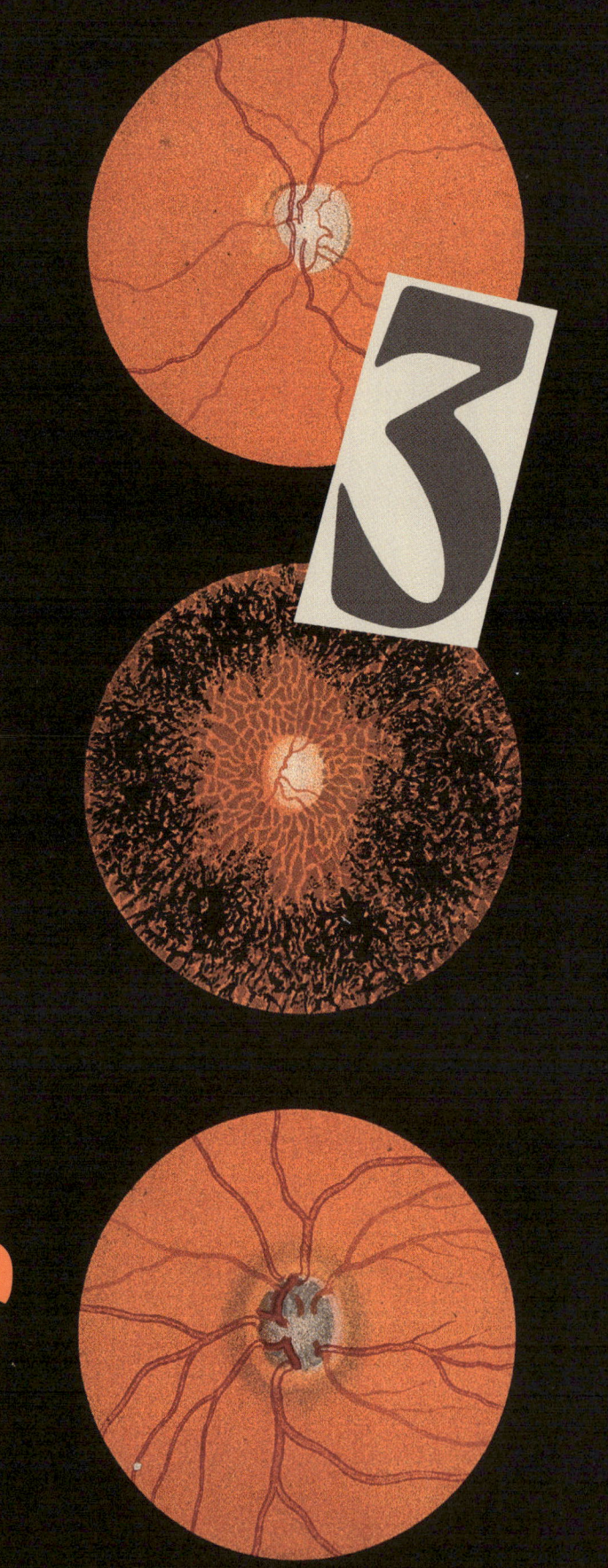

The following essay consists of three interrelated parts of what it might mean for us to think and act as organisations rather than as individuals.

I have attempted to articulate this question through three related but distinct themes. The first concerns the problem of individualism versus the individual. The second speaks more directly to the question of what it might mean to think and act as an organisation. The third part addresses the transnational dimension of political organising. The essay is divided into three parts with an understanding that the length, style of writing, and some of the content demands a lot of patience from the reader. Although the sections have been written in sequence and are intended as a single written essay, I have tried to make it so that each of them can be read individually if desired. I have spoken in the first person throughout. I have done this purposely: individuals should try to shape and influence organisations without over-identifying the organisation's perspective with their own personal one. I did not want to use 'we' or write in the impersonal form because these are my own thoughts which not only aim to influence people outside of Plan C but also try to convince my own comrades within it. It would not make sense to say that in an argument such as this one can 'speak for' an entire organisation, so I have written in the same first-personal form that I would use to relate these ideas in a meeting or an assembly.

1. Individualism and the Individual

Much ink has been spilled over the question of the individual in the modern history of radical left politics. At times, it can become difficult to identify a genuine critique of repression under Real Existing Socialism from the ideological results of anti-communist hysteria in the West. That is, it is difficult in the long shadow of the Cold War to continue to advocate for a form of communism in which *the individual* does not disappear but *individualism* does. A consequence of this aversion is that it can often prove difficult to argue the case against *individualism* in ways that are not perceived as threatening to also abolish *the individual*. This represents a political problem for us not just because the general public feels some queasiness towards any mention of communism, but also because our own ideology and social identities are to some extent themselves an inheritance of this same history of anti-communist hysteria. If one essential part of adopting a Marxist perspective holds that our very language and social practices aren't always obvious to us at the level of everyday practice, then we have good grounds to be suspicious of our own intuitive biases and their practical everyday consequences for the ways

143

we think and act[1]. For reasons that have less to do with poor discipline or personal failures and much more to do with the ways in which we are all inevitably trapped in the net of history and ideology, we ourselves often fail to take note of how our own defence and understanding of the individual sometimes slips into unwitting affirmations of the very idea of individual freedom cherished by neoliberal capital. *We are not aware of this, nevertheless we do it.*

A more concrete illustration may help to unpack this point a little. We often use the phrase 'good politics' in left discourse. We use it sometimes in ways that mean 'how a person or group thinks about and acts out their political ideas' is commendable and something from which we stand to learn. More often, however, this phrase 'good politics' is simply applied to individuals as a kind of identity claim. 'This person has good politics' means nothing more or less than: they agree with me and have proven this affiliation through open declarations of a performative nature. This is not always a bad thing, since it is good to know where our comrades stand. On the other hand, there are some problematic aspects to this use of 'good politics' in a mainly discursive way. For instance, it is easy to espouse 'good politics' and never really act upon them. No doubt many of us have experienced this. There are plenty of people who say good things but never actually do them or even lay down basic conditions for themselves which would allow them to act upon such good beliefs. Some, if not many, aspire to 'good politics' as a self-sufficient value claim about their individual character that does not have to be backed up by anything more than saying the right things to the right audience, perhaps dressing the right way, or observing the correct mannerisms in a social group. It is possible to join a political group and still engage in virtually no meaningful political activity. It is possible to attend political events and open meetings and say political things that one is in no sense responsible for beyond merely having given an opinion. It is possible to have 'good politics' whilst maintaining

---

1. As to why this is an essential part of adopting a Marxist perspective, we can consider the loosely related case of Marx's critique of the value-form. As Marx writes of the value-form determination in volume 1 of Capital: '... whenever, by an exchange, we equate as values our different products, by that very act, we also equate, as human labour, the different kinds of labour expended upon them. We are not aware of this, nevertheless we do it'. In Marx, Karl, and David McLellan. Selected Writings. 2nd ed, Oxford University Press, 2000. p.475. The important point here is that the value-relation itself is something that we do not recognise in our everyday activity, and that it cannot be simply thought out of existence. The fundamental logic of this point is later developed into a Marxist critique of Ideology by thinkers such as Theodor Adorno and Georg Lukács.

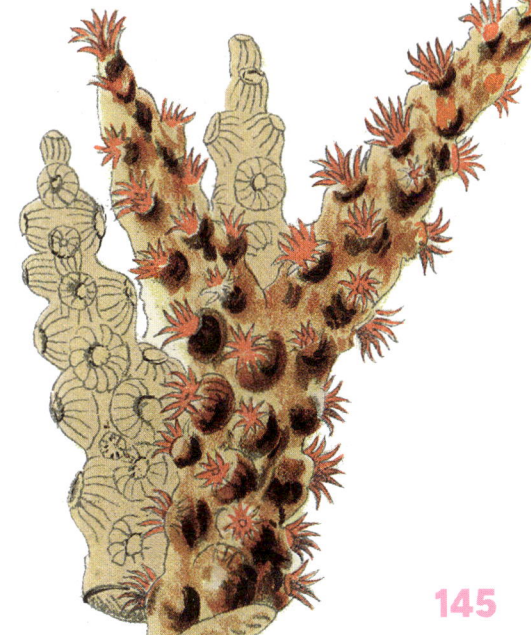

John Augustus Knapp, A Singular Looking Being

reservations about political activity because the right organisation hasn't arrived yet, or because you simply have lost faith and feel 'tired' or 'jaded'. The function of 'good politics' isn't necessarily to exempt us from the difficult demands of political action, but it often serves these ends in practice. If 'good politics' isn't completely about separating thought from practical activity, at very least it tends to privilege opinion over consistent and committed political engagement. It's not that the people who do these things are bad people. The problem is rather that the social and discursive culture of the left often permits us to act in ways that are at odds with what we actually espouse politically. To some extent, all of us are inclined towards and have probably done these things to some degree, not because we are malicious or lazy or stupid, but because the logic of social relations within our own spaces is an inherited logic which we participate in, and which we aren't always capable of recognising.

Of course, individualism has something to do with forms of social atomisation too: material concrete things that a dominant capitalist social order has developed through a series of political decisions which organise proletarian experience in ways that mean it cannot organise itself. The point, once more, is not to say that every time a person says of another that they have 'good politics', they are through an act of ill-discipline fully responsible for reproducing the same system. Inorganic transformations of our language won't get us very far politically speaking, and may on the other hand serve to cultivate a puritanical culture that makes life even more unbearably difficult for left militants than it already is. To be quite direct about this: the point is to transform the social relations, not the language that emerges from them. If we are only interested in transforming the language, we end up simply re-individualising the problem itself. So it will not do to become prescriptive about the way people talk, but perhaps it is strategically valuable for our political orientation to understand why we talk the way we do. As a comrade of mine once put it: 'solutions do not always resemble their problems', a maxim perfectly well-suited to the everyday pitfalls of

John Augustus Knapp, *Each Finger Pointed*

real abstraction apparent here². The

2. The seminal account of 'real abstraction' remains that of Alfred Sohn-Rethel in Sohn-Rethel, A., 1978. Intellectual and Manual Labour: a Critique of Epistemology, Critical Social Studies. Macmillan, London. The very basic outline of this idea is that there are forms of social abstraction which are nevertheless 'real', meaning they are not simply in the head but sustained through concrete forms of activity. The most notable case here is money: it is real, and at the same time it is abstract, it only makes sense insofar as it works at a general social level. Sohn-Rethel's most important claim is to show how such real abstractions determine in some sense the organisation of human experience and the possibility of our knowledge about the world. Put simply: how we think about and experience the world is indelibly shaped by the fact that we use money and cannot help but see everything in terms of monetary relations.

problems inherited from our social relations manifest as symptoms at the level of things like language and culture cannot be resolved merely by cauterising the wounds on language itself, because they are constituted by a materially-embedded logic which remains even if we do correct the terms and manner of our speech. This is one significant sense of what can be meant by 'embracing contradiction', that is: embracing our own inevitable sickness as capitalist subjects in order to better understand its causes, rather than *masking* its symptoms in order to merely appear as ideologically liberated revolutionaries.

'Good politics' is but one particular instance of which there may be many more examples. The reason to contest it here is that as a speech act, it usually only makes sense within the context of a left **social world**[3], and one over-hasty presumption often betrayed by the left's inclination to act as if it is or can be a fully-liberated social sphere that stands above the everyday realities of capitalist domination. We need not say here that this is a consciously-held belief amongst those active in the left. We only need to observe how the existence of the left as a social world, in which certain kinds of etiquette or social performance are treated with disproportionate concern, can *take precedence* over its existence as a **political ecology**[4] composed of various political groups and organisations doing various tangible things. Because these questions of etiquette map on directly to statements of political positions or actions that reveal apparently sound political sensibilities, the prioritisation can seem to be overly concerned with maintaining or 'pruning' the rarefied social space of the left. This brings with it all sorts of negative class connotations that we hardly need to draw out here. Perhaps most importantly, the disproportionate attention paid to value-signifiers that largely only apply to individuals in this context can appear to suggest that real problems of the left are due to various pathogens individuals bring into it through a lack of discipline or some other tragic fault. But it is not simply the case that we take ideology from our lives outside the left into it and thereby contaminate it. Our organisations, our political ecologies, our social world of the left, are themselves all conditioned by and not independent of these ideological afflictions, since they all entail forms of social relation which are also ideologically determined. In fact, it is crucial to recognise that distinguishing between a social world and a political ecology of the left here isn't an either/or question. The left cannot exist without a social world because it also involves social relations. The social world of the left also *should not* exist in a way that is wholly disconnected from the wider social world outside of it. If we exist only as political militants and not also as social individuals, we quickly lose contact with a social base.

It is important to point this out because sometimes the desire to participate in left politics can be motivated by an illusion that we are temporarily exiting from these undesirable forms of capitalist social relation whenever we do so. In this

---

3. I am using the term 'social world' here in a way that will later be differentiated from the idea of a political ecology or organisation. Saying that the left has a social world means that there are certain ideas, ways of speaking, and activities that make sense within it in a purely social, rather than practical political sense. This is not a bad thing as long as the left isn't just or mainly a social world.

4. Political ecology will be defined at length later in this essay, but the basic difference between this idea and that of a social world is that the activity, language and ideas that make sense within a political ecology are in some way incompatible with the state of capitalist society. That is another way of saying that the things people say and do in the context of a political ecology have political consequences, whereas the things people do in a social world have mainly social consequences. These should not be viewed as two distinct realities but different descriptions of the same reality: the social world of the left overlaps strongly with a political ecology of the left, even if not all members of the left social world are meaningfully part of its political ecology. For this reason, it also does not make sense to say that a political ecology can exist in a way that resolves problems arising due to social relations between individuals on the left.

sense, the urge to become politically organised may also function as one particular means of coping with the everyday abrasiveness of capitalist totality. This desire may in turn promote habitual blindness to the ways in which ideology and real abstraction still pervade our thinking and activity even as we inhabit political space. On the one hand, it is true that political organisations realise some practical possibility of living, thinking, and acting differently. The notion of prefiguration—to create the different forms of life we want to engender in a revolutionary society at a more local scale in ways that are often temporary and limited—is entirely operative if understood in this sense. On the other hand, we can only achieve these things imperfectly in our present reality. We disabuse ourselves of any comforting illusions once we begin to reckon with the fact that our experience has been indelibly organised around an implicit set of value-claims, wherein our abstract worth is determined by how our outspoken opinions are perceived and validated by others. These things happen to us, because in so many ways the social infrastructure and reified social relations that govern our lives condition us to think in such terms. We cannot adopt better beliefs or educate ourselves out of this problem, even if doing both of these things is also important and necessary. We also cannot treat left politics as a space in which such capitalist relations are completely suspended, even if our organisations and political ecologies provide us with a space to try and think and act differently and in ways that are critical of capitalist social relations. Once again, if thinking and the space of possible action happens downstream of the real social relations that determine it, then the political project must be to develop the material practices and structures which can ultimately change the ways in which we can think and act beyond any temporary environment created by the left. How our experience is organised is always a matter of something that is *external* to our innermost thoughts. The very terms in which we can think or act are determined by the material conditions in which we live and the social relations they embody. The

John Augustus Knapp, *This Struggling Ray of Sunlight*

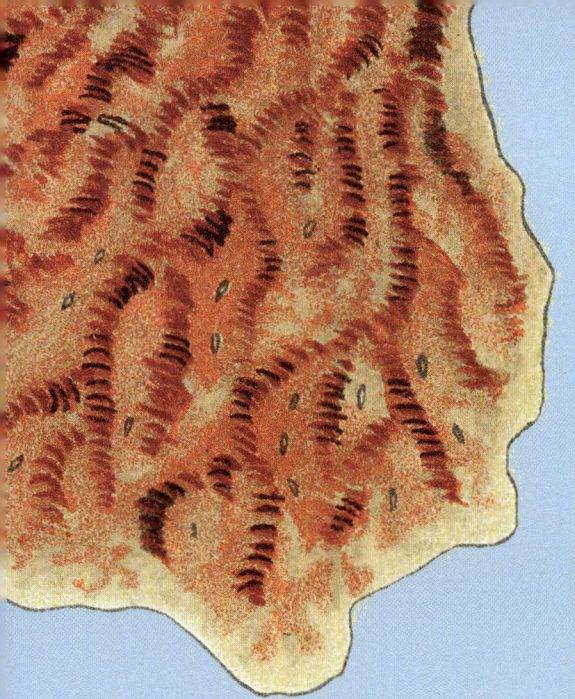

question of political practice is how we can materially go about changing this, which requires not just action for its own sake but **determinate**[5] forms of action which can transform the space of possibility for *both* thought and action.

In light of these observations, we can see how our original question concerning the individual versus individualism has always been poorly posed, still browbeaten by the enduring hangover of the Cold War. It was a mistake to think that it could be resolved as a choice between these mutually opposed political systems, a fact which has surely been proven beyond all doubt by the sham concept of freedom that neoliberalism still works overtime to promote as paramount. As revolutionaries, the issue of how we might navigate this question of individual freedom versus collective need must be answered practically and through forms of conscious deliberation. We should think of such questions not as being answerable in the form of timeless essences, but rather as socially and historically variable. We should expect our received ideas about the meaning of 'individual' or 'collective' in the here and now to be different from what they would look like in a genuinely communist society. A part of what we are trying to do in revolutionary political work is to create the material conditions under which our understanding of these concepts can be transformed, because our social reality itself has been transformed. This is a simple matter of saying that the problems of a classless society are different—and

5. 'Determinate' action here means not only action that is clear and defined, but also suggests something about the process of getting to 'clear and defined' action in a way that also involves a strong sense of political resoluteness. Clarity of vision is not always a good thing in its own right, because we can easily have a clear vision which is totally false or based on wishful thinking or dogmatic assertion of principles regardless of what any honest political reflection tells us. So the idea of determinate forms of action demands that we not only develop a clear vision, but one which is purposive because it relates to a political process of action and reflection that tries in earnest to develop a truthful relationship to the world.

for want of another term 'better'—than the ones we have in our current class-based society. There are ways in which **organisations** and the **political ecologies** they exist within can allow us to critique and transform our social relations, but we should not thereby take the further step of thinking that these afford us some escape from capitalist social relations or exist in ways that are not themselves determined by them. After all, neither organisations nor ecologies exist in some context that is independent from society, even as they maintain a critical relationship towards it. The problem with terms like 'good politics' and the countless other examples like them is that they presuppose a form of individual subjectivation through which our relationship to political life is conditioned. Even if we say that we want to get away from the politics of individualism or individualised experience without completely losing sight of the individual, the problem remains that we have very little practical understanding of what it means to be 'an individual' outside of an individualist context. This problem is ramified wherever our thinking and practice lead us to re-individualise the problem of escaping individualism. Both the urge to think our way out of this conundrum by uncovering what a 'non-individualist individual' might mean, and the impulse to seek out political organisations as a solution to our personal problem, result in a dead end.

This essay began with the problem of the individual because I believe that the very tangible disappointments, frustrations, and hardships wrought by the impoverished form of individual experience remains a site of struggle for revolutionary politics. This is true above all in the sense that practical solidarity is often built upon a foundation of a shared common experience relatable to the level of individual persons. As we have just seen, strategies for thinking about enlightened individual experience outside the constraints

Théophile-Alexandre Steinlen, *On Strike* from *Le Chambourd Socialiste*

of individualism lead to a dead end. The more contentious claim I wish to make here, however, is that these real abstractions of individualism *also distort the ways in which we organise and think through* political organisation. The problem here is that political organisations can often operate and function in ways that essentially *mirror the individual*. We need look no further than the kinds of power-struggles which often take place within political organisations, and how these power struggles try to foreclose the more painstaking discursive practices in favour of a charismatic leader in order to 'get things done'. One example of where we see this is where the distinction between strategic and tactical discussions is blurred. In such cases we often see how the sense of immediacy demanded by quick and tactical decision-making on the ground seeps into the more deliberative and measured discussion required for political strategising in meetings. Affectations of extreme urgency in these discussions can have the effect of circumventing the sometimes lengthier deliberative process demanded when working through complex political problems. In creating a general sense that there is no time for deliberation, the person who conflates these two distinct political contexts can often claim a degree of authority. Since decisions on the ground don't allow for the same degree of horizontality, they tend to recommend more clearly defined hierarchical roles specific to that context. It is not hard to see how deliberately creating a sense that the same urgency applies to all political situations can end up pushing us into assenting to the authoritative voice of one or two individuals in a political organisation. This blurring of contexts can lead to the entrenchment of more permanent hierarchies, as opposed to the situation-dependent and in many cases interchangeable hierarchical roles that may be required in

contexts of direct action. This is just one example amongst many which should be seen not only as types of individualist syndrome, but perhaps more importantly, as **symptomatic of a failure of organisations themselves to act organisationally**. A blurring of the boundaries of what kind of activity is taking place in what context that leads the *political* organisation to deteriorate into a largely *social* one.

We can generalise this kind of problem by pointing to the fact that many people's relationship to political organisations still bears the character of being a useful appendage to one's own political will. Whereas collective learnings through material practice can be encoded within a form of organisational memory reproduced by healthy patterns of internal discourse, an organisation whose function becomes distorted as it is subordinated to the individual will can only harness as much of this knowledge and reflection as seems important to that select group of individuals. Not only does the space of political thought and action latent within the political organisation shrink to a fraction of its potential when processes of thinking and acting are shrunken to the whims of a small number of charismatic individuals' whims, but pretty soon the possibility of transforming or reformatting our own experience through radical political militancy also begins to diminish. Without needing to spell out all of the ways in which this can happen, just consider for instance how quickly the social division of labour is restored when one or two individuals assume or assert control over the political organisation. How often, indeed, do the very structures that create incentives to pathologically seek attention, to struggle for power, to have one's personal wishes and projects realised through the labour of others end up representing the same forms of discourse and practice which we would otherwise think of as synonymous with the condition of individualism?

An objection here may be that I have already assumed an extent to which individualist culture always pervades the political organisation under conditions of capitalist domination. This is indeed true, but does not mean that there is nothing we can do to mitigate it. The entire purpose of recognising the extent to which these tendencies continue to permeate even the most radical left organisations is not to see them as an inalterable fact of nature. It is instead to say that a basic recognition of this fact and the particular ways in which it expresses itself within political organisation is a necessary precondition for confronting our constraints and limitations. The problem is not that we are hopelessly condemned to individualist forms of thought and practice. It is that there is a labour of struggling against this which is not overcome by merely joining a left political organisation.

To think and act as organisations, demands first and foremost that we cannot go on thinking as if political organisations are manifestations of the messianic will of the experienced and charismatic and perhaps also confrontational (or indeed as the case may be, the cynically non-confrontational) individual. But how precisely we can address this comes down to a question of practice, not merely agreement with the principle. The crux of antiauthoritarian politics is not a radically horizontal form of organisation, but the very thinking of organisation from a communist standpoint itself. The figure of the supposedly benevolent dictator will always win the efficiency trade-off against these organisational questions if we continue to think that achieving our political goals is merely a matter of 'winning power' or 'getting things done' without examining the question of how that power is constituted or what is to be done. There may be situations in which nested hierarchies are necessary, mainly in specific contexts of political action where quick decisions must be made, where less deliberation is possible, and where we defer to assigned roles of responsibility. Thinking organisationally is the best tool we have to avoid generalising this in ways that are politically harmful and regressive, because it allows us to better define the appropriate scenarios and contexts to which different aspects of the organisation's function are appropriately suited. For this reason, it is important that we see the very question of political efficiency as something tied to the practical possibilities of organisational thinking. Results of any kind can more easily be obtained in the short-run if we simply allow ourselves to act in a way that sees the organisational as a larger version of an individual, such that one or two people act as the head, others as the hands and arms and feet and so on. The problem is that this measure of success ultimately resounds in gratification on an individual level, in the same kind of symbolic way that matters to individuals who care about whether they are perceived, or perceive others, to have 'good politics'. It is, ultimately, a *therapeutic* approach to political life, even when it achieves results that are a little more than therapeutic. The significance of an organisational point of view is that it also transforms our metrics of success, from an 'I did this!', to a point of view that concerns the reproduction and expansion of the organisation and by extension the political niches that it tries to influence both within a broader political ecology and in society at large.

John Augustus Knapp, *With Fear and Trembling*

Peter Newell, *The Startled Swarm*

2. The Organisation

Having outlined in some detail both the quandary of individualism in the context of communist politics and defined the notion of organisational thinking in a *negative* sense, it now becomes necessary to address the subject of organisational thinking in a *positive* sense. Before putting some basic ideas on the table, it would be remiss not to first mention here that much of the thinking and approach of this essay in general, and this section in particular, is derived from the work of Subset of Theoretical Practice (STP), a political research group in which I have actively participated for a number of years. STP's theoretical research is also put to the test practically by organisational work a number of its members carry out with the Common Space of Organisations (CSO)[6]. Much of CSO's work involves connecting organisations through forms of *organisational inquiry* which are closely linked to the principles of workers inquiry. The theoretical work of STP and the practical work of CSO are closely linked and mutually informative. There is not enough space here to do more than cherry-pick some elements of these groups to substantiate the argument I wish to make. The intention is rather to think with and through the framework of STP to address the initial problem I have set up in the previous section, and then to apply these ideas more directly to a field of political activity that Plan C is heavily invested in, namely that of Transnational political struggle, in the final part. To avoid an excessive amount of footnotes, I have opted here to recommend the reader to the *Atlas of Experimental Politics*[7] and

Working Through Political Organisation[8] for a more comprehensive overview of the group's work. References to STP's concepts and thoughts as outlined in these two texts will be interwoven throughout. A more accessible text that outlines the basics of STP's framework and connects it to the experimental practice of CSO is currently being prepared by the group and will be available in English in the near future.

We can now turn our focus more directly towards the question of what an organisation is, or what thinking organisationally means, as opposed to what it does not mean. The answer to this question is not entirely simple, and the present essay will not provide the reader with any kind of formula that can be followed in order to correct some of the problems

6. See: https://www.espacocomum.org/eco-en
7. https://www.sum.si/journal-articles/atlas-of-experimental-politics
8. https://www.crisiscritique.org/storage/app/media/nov-25/subset-of-theoretical-practice.pdf

identified in what has already been outlined above. Instead, the idea is to provide some concepts that can, with some practice, allow us to habituate ourselves to a form of organisational practice. In other words, the purpose here is not to tell organisations what they ought to do, but to try to open up a kind of perspective within which it may be possible to imagine the various problems and challenges we face differently. It is better to think in terms of a toolkit than a recipe or set of orders to be adhered to.

Firstly, we can think about organisations in the sense of **political organisations**. That is, most likely, the kinds of organisations that many on the political left will either be a part of or have been a part of or wish to be a part of. Many different kinds of political organisations may be considered revolutionary here and there is no uniformity between them. We can arbitrarily group certain 'types' of revolutionary organisation together to whatever extent it can help us to understand what our **political ecology** looks like and the different roles various organisations play within it. That being said, these distinctions should not be taken as final or absolute, and the majority of organisations will incorporate a variety of different approaches into the way they work, strategise, and understand themselves. Some political organisations adopt a more general revolutionary outlook and develop a political strategy in multiple fields of struggle according to this outlook. Examples of this type of organisation might include Plan C or a revolutionary left political party or any Marxist political group. In other cases, a political organisation starts from a more narrowly defined field of activity, more clearly defined goals, and a more 'direct' strategy for achieving its goals. Examples of such groups may include base

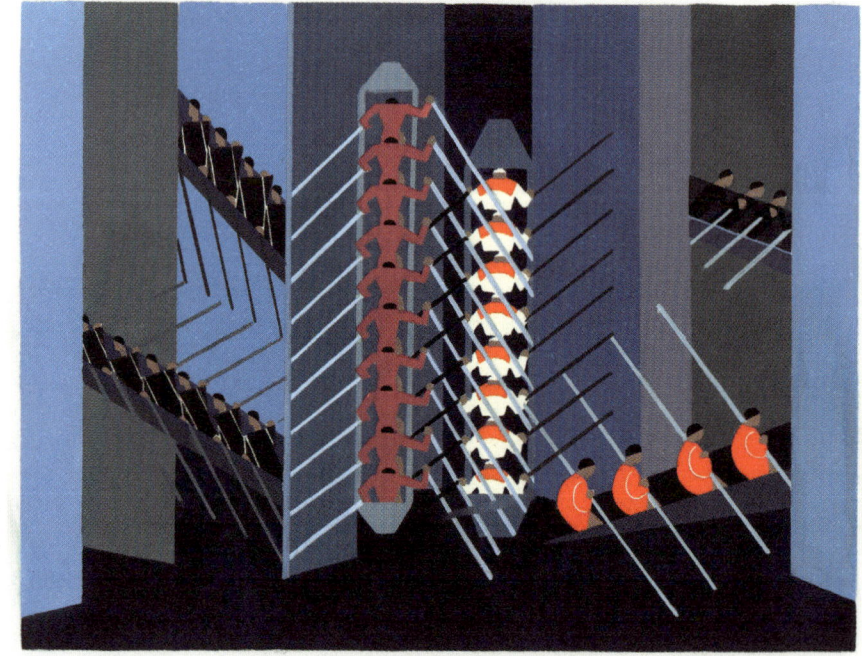

Alexandra Exter, *Maquette de Théatre IX*

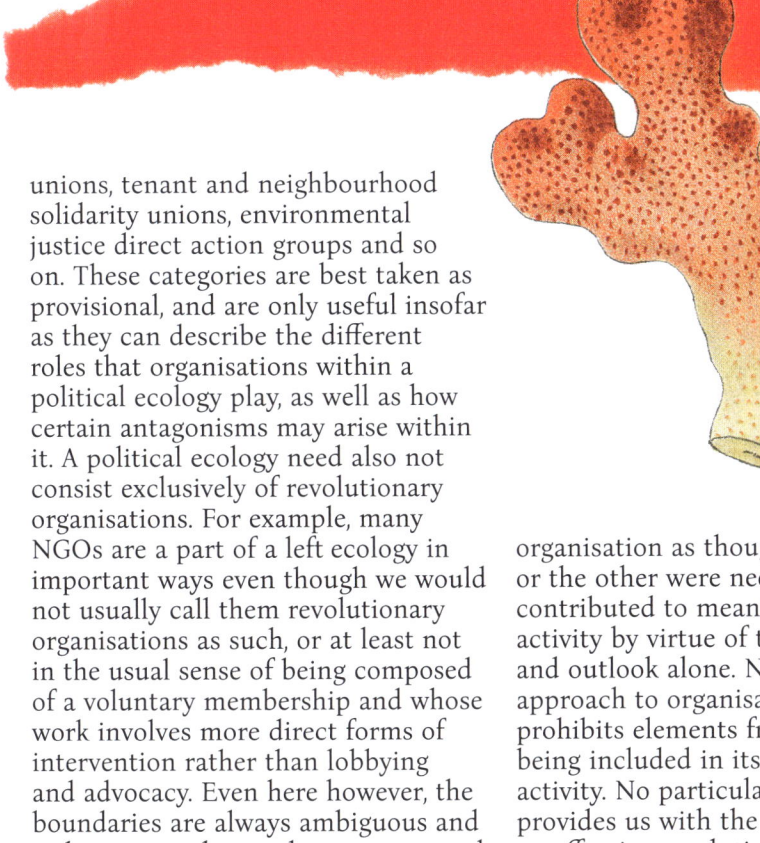

unions, tenant and neighbourhood solidarity unions, environmental justice direct action groups and so on. These categories are best taken as provisional, and are only useful insofar as they can describe the different roles that organisations within a political ecology play, as well as how certain antagonisms may arise within it. A political ecology need also not consist exclusively of revolutionary organisations. For example, many NGOs are a part of a left ecology in important ways even though we would not usually call them revolutionary organisations as such, or at least not in the usual sense of being composed of a voluntary membership and whose work involves more direct forms of intervention rather than lobbying and advocacy. Even here however, the boundaries are always ambiguous and it does not make much sense to spend our time trying to police them. It may be perfectly reasonable to say of some NGOs that they work in quite similar ways to revolutionary organisations and in many ways can be considered as a political organisation in disguise. In any case, there is only so much we can say at this level of generality, and the more important point is that every organisation should seek to understand both itself and the other groups it works with as fulfilling certain functions within the context of a political ecology.

A great deal of time and energy has been wasted in comparing the merits of different forms of political organisation as though only one or the other were necessary or contributed to meaningful political activity by virtue of their form and outlook alone. No particular approach to organisational form prohibits elements from others from being included in its organisational activity. No particular field of struggle provides us with the key to building an effective revolutionary movement. No particular strategy or set of tactics will prove successful across all relevant contexts. Organisations that dedicate less time to thinking and reflective activity are not in error if the demands of how that organisation functions means that allocating such high importance to this kind of task would not make sense. This should not be generalised as a critique of other organisations which *do* see it as worthwhile in their context to engage in such things. An organisation with a very general political outlook can engage in specific political projects whilst also consistently maintaining a practice of theoretical reflection and discussion. It can do this without advancing the idea that it has found the truly enlightened form of political organisation and set an example which all others should follow. Plan C, for instance, should seek to try and influence other organisations in its political ecology by sharing ideas and allowing other organisations to draw from its political and organisational practices whatever is useful to them. It should not, on the other hand, seek to do this by trying to transform every organisation in its ecology into something that thinks, acts, and looks like Plan C. Not only would this likely fail, but would also be a grave *strategic* error.

Internecine conflicts surrounding these questions often take place amongst individual members of an organisation as well as between different organisations. Often this becomes a competition between egos, where individuals seek to assert their authority or political nous by claiming that the particular strategic or tactical approach their organisation takes can be generalised as *the* revolutionary strategy which all others must follow. The knock-on effect of this can be disastrous, leading to a corrosive effect on the relationships between organisations where individuals within them feel condescended to, disrespected by, or resentful of others who claim to have a more enlightened understanding of what it would take to instigate a revolution than they themselves do. But beyond the deleterious effects on the relationships between organisations, this view must also be pathologised as a social behaviour that has very little to do with real politics, and which ends up being actively unhelpful in many cases even as far as strategy is concerned. As discussed in the opening part of this essay, these assertions around whose

Albert Robida, *Transatlantic Balloon*, from *Le Vingtième Siècle*

approach to political organisation is the 'best' or 'most effective' often overly personalise political problems and questions. The idea that there is or can be some 'silver bullet' where it comes to organisational form or strategy is more often than not an indication that someone has failed to apprehend the political ecology of which the organisation is a part, instead seeking to strongly identify the ecology itself with a single organisation and its form.

Political ecology is the second important concept which we need to spell out here. Rodrigo Nuñez has provided an excellent overview of this idea of a political ecology[9], one also largely adopted by STP. This essay will only cover some aspects of this concept whose far richer meaning can be found in both Nuñez's texts and in the aforementioned work of STP. The basic sense in which I am using the idea here concerns the way in which political organisations in a shared context *interact with* and *see* each other. It also has to do with the idea that there is a shared **political context**[10] between these organisations.

---

9. See: Nunes, Rodrigo. Neither Vertical nor Horizontal: A Theory of Political Organisation. Verso Books, 2021.

10. The basic thought behind this concept of a shared political context is that political groups share such a context to the extent that they do political work in the same social or material context. Two different groups can have strong political affinities but share no or only a very weak political context, i.e. they exist in different territories. A shared political context is something that can be built, for example through transnational struggle in this

One very important way in which a *political* ecology differs from a *social* world is that in the case of the latter, the shared concepts, understanding, and reality of the *political* ecology are incompatible with the usual order of the society in which it exists. In other words, within a shared *political* ecology the way we act and the language we use as individuals and organisations reflects a shared understanding that the world is not in the order we would like it to be. As Rafael Saladanha helpfully puts it: political activity which is *incompatible* with the dominant logic of a given society is *compatible* with that of a political ecology[11]. This shared critical perspective on the world is what allows us to have a shared sense of reality even if we do not share a political perspective or strategy. It means that we can talk to, see, and make sense of each others' actions in ways that are not immediately coherent to those outside of the political ecology.

A political ecology can, as the term suggests, be likened to an ecosystem in which organisations are capable of seeing and interacting with one another. This ecosystem is in some sense itself *organised*, although not always in ways that are explicitly visible. The concept of political ecology is useful for thinking about the form of political organisation insofar as different organisations engaged in different forms of political practice at different sites can coordinate with one another, rather than compete with one another to assert the supremacy of their particular form and political practice.

To think in terms of political ecology does not imagine one great federated union of organisations along the left. It steers clear of any 'left unity' fantasy, where the kind of unity being imagined is one in which every other organisation in the ecosystem looks like and acts according to the demands of the organisation asserting theirs as the appropriate framework under which to unify. Political ecologies should not be seen as the final framework for political cohesion. It is, of course, the objective of revolutionary left organisations to dissolve themselves precisely at the point where there is no meaningful distinction between a left ecology and society at large. We can imagine that a stronger sense of cohesion would be required in a world where our organisations have transformed themselves into or are replaced by communist social structures that provide for the needs our current political activity illuminates in some critical way.

A significant benefit of acting in the context of a political ecology is that it allows us to take account of which other groups may have traction in political contexts where our own does not, or which may have the skills and tools to accomplish certain activities which our own organisation lacks. It makes possible the act of generating political ideas and activity without necessarily imposing the question of 'how does our organisation achieve this?' upon individual groups in every case. The idea is not entirely new, but its formalisation as a *habit* is what changes once we understand this form of activity within the rubric of *thinking organisationally*. **Political ecologies make possible certain affordances that political organisations alone do not possess, just as political**

---

case.
11. See: https://space.ideaofcommunism.comuploads/7d8a80d22e1c3a08b4181d2852115b20.pdf

organisations make possible certain things that individuals alone, no matter how 'good' their politics may be, cannot achieve. Finally, to more explicitly understand our organisations as part of ecologies often means that we organically begin to think and understand our own organisation in organisational terms. That is to say: we develop a clearer sense of what our own organisation is, what it can do, what it could do if certain things were changed or developed in a certain direction, and also by *seeing what it is not* in the context of a political ecology. We can understand where our strengths lie by measuring our practical efforts not in terms of how they measurably disrupt the state and capital alone, but rather in terms of how they contribute to a political ecology and much broader range of political forces whose combined efforts across different sites, using different approaches, in relation to different aspects of capital's own organisation, contribute to revolutionary activity.

As we go through the various levels of the question of organisation, we can also begin to see how ecologies are themselves in some sense 'organised' in one way or another, and in ways that can be described as better or worse. On one hand, a political ecology is not a political organisation and cannot be treated as one. We cannot decide to found a political ecology in the same way we can decide to found a political organisation or group. On the other hand, the notion of a political ecology is something constructed in the sense that it can be named and described, as well as in the sense that it can be expanded through the activity of building shared political contexts and relationships with groups who are not already included within it. Understanding how our political ecologies map onto the social ecology also allows us to see where there may be gaps, where either no active political groups exist within an important field of struggle or where such groups do exist but are virtually isolated from the left political ecology at large. This observation highlights a more

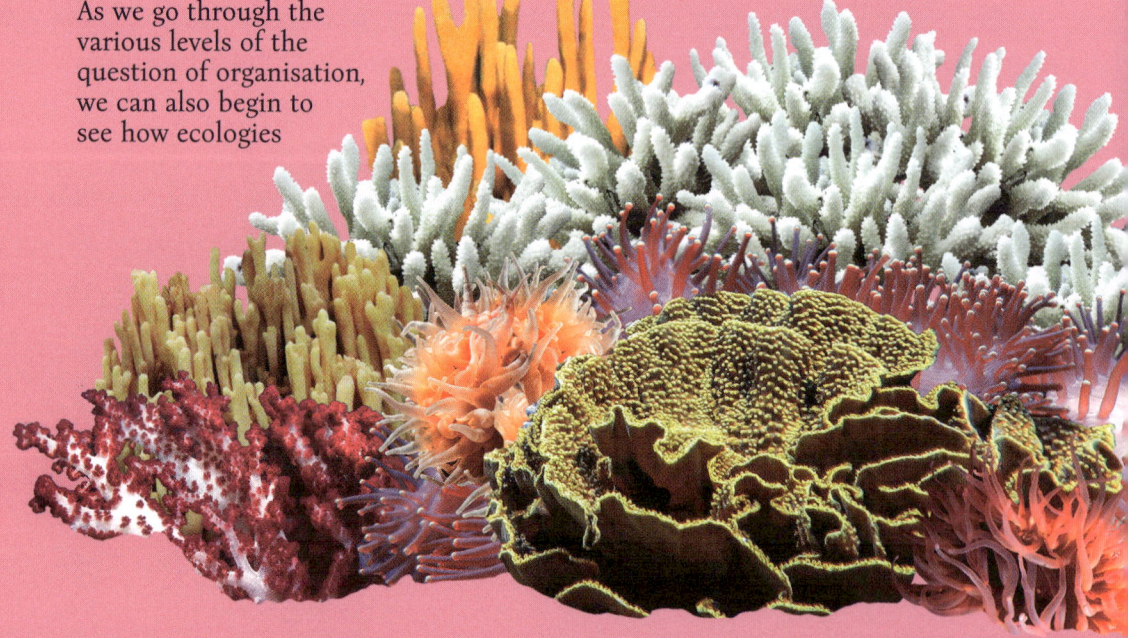

important point about the nature of organisation, namely, that organisation is a more general thing that can be studied, and the relevant questions of organisation are not limited to the question of what form our own political organisation takes. In other words, thinking organisationally does not simply mean thinking about how our own organisations are structured, how they reproduce themselves, it also means thinking about how they function in a larger context that is also organised in some way or another. Two further points abound from this one: firstly, that the system of capital and state to which communist organisations are opposed is *also* organisationally composed in ways that can be made discernable through material interactions and analysis, and secondly, that when taken as this more general principle, there are multiple scales at which organisation can be understood, and that it is ultimately possible to say that the entire social world which we inhabit is organised in some particular way rather than another.

STP's organisational approach is strongly motivated by this connection between organisations as the collective entity in which political militants participate to the more general sense in which the world itself amounts to a form of organisation which is at least partially discernable, can be interacted with, and which **decomposes** into particular smaller forms of organisation. We can in principle understand any given state, for instance, as a coagulation of different parts that are interdependent and interactive with one another. This is another way of saying that it is organised in a particular way, and from this it follows that it can be decomposed into constituent organisational parts, each of which in turn have their own organisational form and function. To say that any state is organised here rather than not does not mean that the way it is

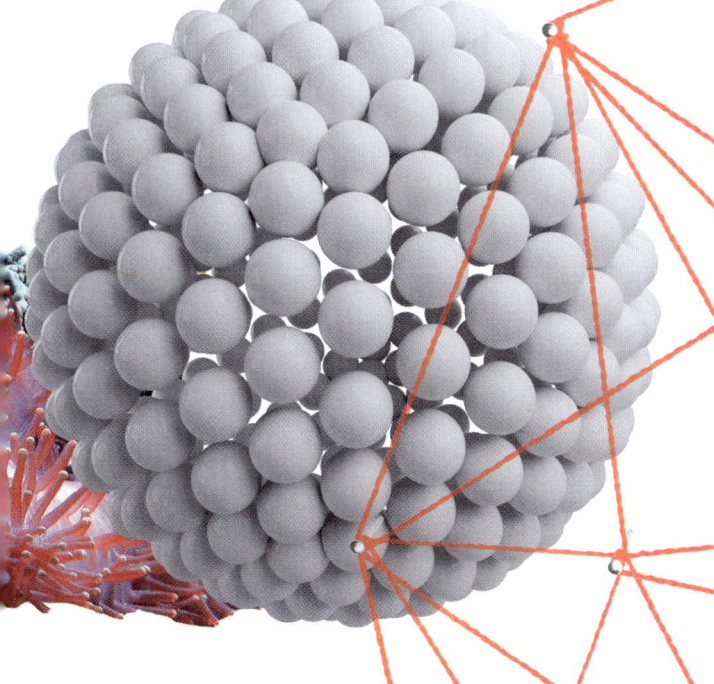

organised in every sense is a conscious act of the state, or that the ways in which it is organised is something intelligible to the state from a singular point of view. In particular, an organisational point of view demands that we develop a more precise and determinate approach wherever we wish to speak about 'strategy' or 'tactics', rather than degenerate into grand narratives and abstractions which more often lend themselves to a sense of 'the big idea'. The point is not that we should never have any kind of narrative or always avoid abstraction in our attempts to understand the world. It is rather that the reality of effective political action demands more precise forms of orientation and a fine-grained approach which is not expressible through these broader vocabularies more attuned to the level of general ideas. Using once more the idea of the state: it is not really possible to act politically against 'the state' in the sense that we often speak of it to mean a very general abstraction which groups together a large number of institutions and functions. The state itself is composed of many different functional parts, a number of which do not even fully understand or interact with each other. Understanding *how* the state is itself organised can also reveal facts about how it functions without the state itself even being conscious that it functions in such a particular way. This can be seen wherever, for instance, the court system is used to undermine the function of police or government. On the other hand, parts of the state may interact with and be highly interdependent upon one another in ways that are also important for us to know when it comes to the real possibility of political action against it. This means to pay attention to precisely how the state is organised, to draw attention to the different things that compose it, to understand it not as a fully coordinated and conscious entity but as a form of organisation about which we can discover certain things about *how* it is organised through political action that interacts with it.

The question of how our political organisations are **composed** is not merely a question of class, gender, racial, or other compositions to do with identity features of the members, but also the very structural questions about how the organisation functions and what kinds of social base it

1

connects to. Of course, the actual identity composition of the members of an organisation *is* highly relevant to this question too. If an organisation is mainly composed of members of a certain social class or race or gender, then its ability to engage in certain fields of struggle by connecting with a social base not represented in some way within its ranks will often prove futile. This is not to say that organisations must incorporate social bases into themselves in order to effectively organise in those contexts, and in many ways the need for taking the view of political ecologies rather than limiting our political horizon to political organisations also recommends that the question of 'who we work with' need not always best be answered by trying to artificially subsume certain groups into our own social space. It should still concern organisations if their current composition is largely skewed in favour of certain identity positions and the perspectives that go with them. If an organisation is mostly made up of white members, it *should* be asking questions about why this is the case. However, an additional benefit of taking the view of political ecologies and acting as an organisation in relation to them is that the shift within organisational space and culture can often happen more spontaneously and the composition problems solved less by heavy-handed and tokenising membership initiatives. If an organisation's political strategy involves organising as well as building and maintaining relations of practical solidarity with a racialised minority population in its own territory, it would do better to identify the ways in which that social group is already organised and attempt to build affinity with it rather than to go into such communities with a party recruitment strategy. This is a far more fruitful approach because it means that the organisation as a whole can learn more directly from how members of this social community organise themselves, and thereby transform their own internal cultures and methodologies in ways that make organising together far more compatible. At the same time,

Théophile-Alexandre Steinlen, *The Next Session* from *Le Chambourd Socialiste*

the field of composition within an organisation is also often a site of struggle. Where the composition of an organisation is diverse, it may also mean that its members are differently situated with respect to parts of the capitalist social world. Wage discrepancies or occupation may allow some members to engage in greater levels of political activity or take greater personal risks than others. Rather than allowing such differences to degenerate into an individualising logic of resentment and neuroticism, it is important to work through these differences in the context of refining the reproductive and other needs of the organisation in ways that are sensitive to its compositional features. That can mean that organisations pay greater heed to the material and social needs of specific members in order to better facilitate the possibility of militant activity, which is always and for the vast majority of people frustrated in one way or another by the ways in which they must participate in capitalist society. The point of understanding composition here is partly to understand precisely *how* people are oppressed in a variety of ways. There is no singular answer or moral value schema that allows us to navigate these things, but rather a set of concrete organisational questions: what forms of action are we capable of, what do we need to do to reproduce each other? How do we understand each other's needs in ways that are not understood as a generic and universal account of need?

It is equally important to understand how an organisation is composed from the point of view of how it *functions* or can function. This is to say that there are different kinds of things that the organisation can do or not do depending on how it is internally organised, what kinds of skills and abilities people have, how many active members it has, how it manages to reproduce itself and so forth. One way to understand how an organisation is composed is to learn from how it has been *decomposed* in cases where problems arise for which there are no immediate solutions. The emergence of problems within a political organisation can be viewed in a positive light when we take an organisational point of view. When everything functions well, there is no real reason to pay attention to the question of how things fit together or in what way they are composed. But it should in some way be a consistent feature of any revolutionary political organisation that it is not characterised by complete stability in how it functions. This is not meant in an absolute sense, where the ideal function of a revolutionary organisation is one characterised by cycles of total collapse and rebuild. However counter-intuitive this may seem, isolated local breakdowns within the various parts of a revolutionary organisation are often a sign of positive development. Adding new members representing a more diverse range of identity groups should create certain frictions which in the best cases lead organisations to revise their previous practices and structures. An increase in membership size may lead to a breakdown in established decision-making processes in such a way that resolving the issue leads to a positive political learning. It is not a guarantee that decomposition alone will lead to positive outcomes. Just as we can say that there are many dysfunctional social institutions which are susceptible to numerous cases of breakdown but limp on with the aid of only the most perfunctory solutions, we can also identify this risk

Alexandra Exter, *Maquette de Théatre VI*

in the case of political organisations. Moments of decomposition are useful insofar as they allow us to understand how our organisations are composed, but this fact alone should not be taken as a substitute for the political task of reflecting on what these moments tell us and employing appropriate corrective measures. The way in which this is done and the extent to which it is treated as a political problem is in some sense a distinguishing feature of revolutionary political organisations.

In relation to our outward political activity and the way in which capital itself composes, the material and social forms of support that allow it to produce and reproduce itself in specific fields of struggle that we operate in, we can also very usefully apply this same principle. A strike is a very effective way of showing the composition and function of a particular mode of production as well as how this form of production or reproduction functions as part of larger social organisation and its composition. When that mode of production suddenly stops running as expected, its compositional and functional realities become visible in ways that they may previously not have been to the vast majority of people. A strike by public transport workers suddenly calls the entire compositional unity of a metropolis into question, it draws attention to the question of what is materially needed in order for things to function. We must also draw attention here to the fact that the ways in which members of a society interact with public transport workers suddenly changes from the very moment at which they stop working and the network breaks down as a result.

This once more illuminates the sense in which the everyday operation of a society is composed, the kinds of interactions and social relations that are necessary for it to operate smoothly and reliably. When it comes to political organisation, this equally holds true. In order to effect a perspective of thinking organisationally rather than individually, we must maintain sight of how the organisation is composed in this sense, not just as a matter of which groups are represented, but also how the organisational structure creates relations between its different militants, how certain activities and functions are carried out by certain members and so on. This may yield various recommendations that lead us to organise ourselves differently and in ways that are more robust to different failure scenarios. It should give us a better sense of what we, as an organisation, are capable of doing, in such a way that strategic and tactical conversations are not hamstrung by the very general demands of individuals concerning 'what is to be done', often themselves totally insensitive

to what the organisation or its wider ecology are actually capable of doing given their real composition. There is no point at which the composition of an organisation is fully or adequately understood, both because the organisation should continue to change both in terms of its membership and also because the relevant features of composition and relation are not exhaustive, and vary according to context. It is just a matter of saying that we never finally know in some definitive sense what our organisation is made up of or what it can achieve as a result, but rather, **thinking as an organisation entails a constant process of working this out through the practical activity of the organisation**.

It is trivially true that the site of political activity is organisational. That is not to dispute the claim that the personal is also political, but the reason we join organisational formations is through a realisation that whatever we might hope to achieve politically cannot be achieved through individual actions alone. Some of the pitfalls here have already been mentioned above, by highlighting the particular problematic sense in which this can lead individuals to see organisations as a mass of undifferentiated labour power that will enable them to affect their own particular projects and designs about how the world should organise itself or capital can be subverted. It has been mentioned already that this somehow undermines or subverts the true potential of the political organisation itself, but it is important to follow up on this claim by giving some sense of how this is the case. I have just outlined a very brief and somewhat syncretic notion of composition in the above. This is one of three parts of what STP has termed 'organisational trinitarianism', a triadic structure relating to the organisational point of view which comprises three basic features of organisation: **composition**, **interaction**, and **intelligibility**. A brief look at the latter two of these will help us to understand the distinction between an organisation acting more cohesively as an organisation, and the aforementioned case where an organisation acts largely dysfunctionally and as an appendage of the charismatic individual.

Firstly, an organisation interacts with flows and processes of capital at a given number of sites or contexts. Its interaction with these flows of capitalist activity allows the organisation to understand in some deeper sense *how* capital operates and is composed in this specific context, rather than merely understanding *that* it does. The **interaction** between political organisations and capital in their given contexts is experimental in the sense that it acts materially according to some informed hypothesis about how capitalist power functions. It observes the consequences of this action, and it thereby learns something both about the composition, structure, and power of capital in both its material and social sense with respect to this context, and *also* about its own composition and power. Through consolidating the results of this material and experimental interaction with capital through forms of political action, the organisation can engage in enduring forms of political and organisational activity out of which a more refined strategy and tactical arsenal can emerge. In doing this, it creates a **political context** within which to act, and this political context can to some degree be shared with other organisations, through coalitions, affinity groups, knowledge and skill sharing and so forth. **Determinate** political action turns not upon the ability to show off how pragmatic-minded a group or organisation is, deprecating the role of theory or reflection as a result. Determinate political action demands a degree of consistency that understands the truth of material practice as the ultimate effectuation of political thought. This is indelibly an act of hypothesis testing: we develop a certain conviction, we put that conviction into practice, we examine the extent to which it is true, we thereby incorporate it into our understanding of the world and capital not in a conceptual sense but in a sense that decomposes into real processes of production and reproduction at both the social and material level. Once again, it is the difference between our knowing *how* and knowing *that*.

Intelligibility is intimately connected to this idea of interaction. Whereas interaction describes the moment in which we practically interact with things, intelligibility describes the process through which the results of this action are incorporated into a wider understanding and operational sensibility that enables us to navigate the world as political organisations. It allows us to see precisely *how* different things are connected and not simply know *that* they are connected or interdependent. It is the difference between using an everyday object like a computer and understanding *how* a computer actually works. Importantly, there are a number of different senses in which we can answer this question of 'how a computer actually works', for instance, from the perspective of hardware: the extraction of raw materials, assembly of the motherboard and silicone chips, its physical housing and display features, and then also in terms of software: operating system, network protocols, applications written in different coding languages and so on. We should assume that all of these are potentially relevant layers of description that correspond to the question of *how* things work, meaning that a diverse range of different interactions at different sites or in relation to different compositions of capital are always valuable in one way or another. Simultaneously, the intelligibility of capital and its various compositional structures can always be assessed in ways that are relevant to the different scales and resolutions at which they appear. We come to understand these things by interacting with capital at sites of struggle, and intelligibility refers to the way in which this information is in some sense organised such that we can both understand and practically navigate our social world, engaging in revolutionary political strategy that is sensitive to this activity and what it tells us about the world as a result.

What this has to do with organisations is just the fact that it is not individuals but organisations which take on this kind of activity in ways which are most effective. We should think about this in a way that is entirely analogous to labour in industrial and post-

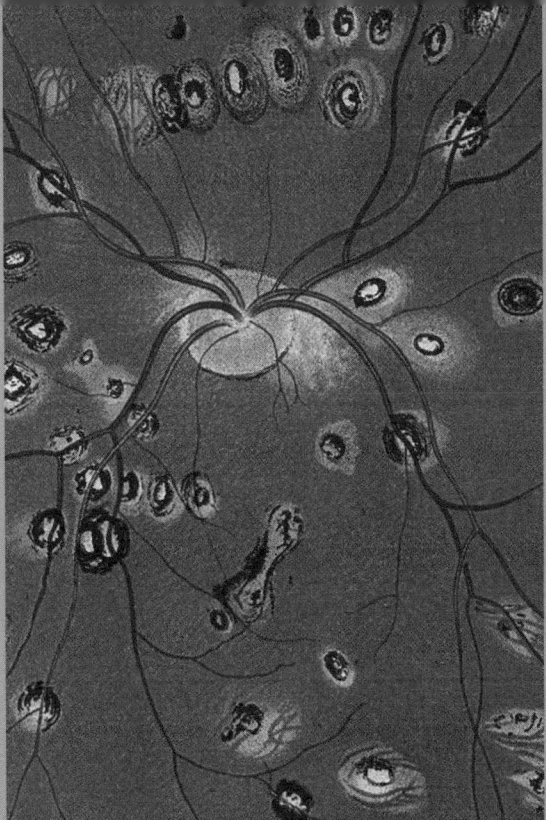

industrial societies. This labour which can in some very crucial sense be distinguished from individual craftsmanship, is always divided up into specialised tasks. Individuals understand their task and responsibility in a specialised way that gives them a very precise sense of how that specific part of a larger whole which they are engaged in producing operates. They can and more often will carry out this activity without having an understanding of how the whole itself functions. On the other hand, there are of course specialists whose role it is to understand the functional unity of the objects of production. We can think here about aircraft engineers, who must understand in intricate detail what every part of an airplane does, how things work in relation to one another, diagnose problems through a very practical rather than merely theoretical understanding of this combined and synchronous function of parts. Even these specialists, however, do not necessarily know how to pilot the plane, they cannot be entrusted to carry out air-traffic control operations, they probably won't know how to correctly follow safety and hospitality protocols that the cabin crew are tasked with, they don't know how to extract the minerals and other raw materials that the parts of the aircraft are made of or how to assemble them into the parts that they know so well and operate with. We can enumerate several more aspects of such organisational activity that are essential to the entire productive operation that allows even a single airplane to fly from one location to another. The upshot is that it is only possible to accomplish such activities within an organisational context. Without this organisation, expressing the idea that one needs to fly from one place to another in order to save vast amounts of time is as meaningful as demanding the existence of teleportation to satisfy the same need.

We should understand our political organisations in the same vein: in ways that might require many specialised functions, which consolidate practical knowledge through forms of interactive experimentation, political production and reproduction, that are consolidated into forms of knowledge and practical intelligibility

Alexandra Exter, *Divadelný Návrh XIII*

that are available not just to one individual but are captured by the organisation as a whole. When we raise frustrations about 'doing things', about the possibility of a form of political activity that is in any way adequate to the structure of the world we are confronted with, it is perhaps this **mismatch between the organisational sophistication of the world and that of our own political organisations which leads to such constant despair and frustration**. What is being proposed here may equally seem like an enormous if not impossible task, given that the forms of production and social production which now exist and make up the composition of the world we live in are developed and structured through the very forms of life and organisation that have been in motion for centuries. Moreover, they are produced and upheld through the mute compulsion[12] of capitalist social relations: we simply must sell our labour as proletarians to survive, we are bound to a capitalist form of activity and the logic that goes with it as a basic question of survival and materially reproducing ourselves. An abrupt and discomfiting truth we must also face is that there is often neither enough time nor an appropriate social context allowing us to engage in forms of activity that are *not* remunerated in the form of wages or coordinated according to the organisational logic of capital. We may then rightly ask how the kinds of complex and sophisticated kinds of political organisation being recommended here are even possible,

---

12. 'Mute compulsion' refers to the way in which economic power enforces participation in capital by having control over the processes of social life. Soren Mau's 2023 book Mute Compulsion is well worth the read for anyone seeking a deeper analysis of this topic.

given that we are disadvantaged in respect of time, given that so much of the world is already shaped by the path dependencies engendered by the value relation, and given that we exist in a context where capital and state power actively militates against our capacity to organise.

There is no easy or consoling answer to this question, but a shift away from one conventionally-held perspective is quite necessary when confronting such a difficult reality. Namely, it is better not to understand anti-capitalist revolution as a complete *abolition* of capitalist modernity—understood as a totality of social and material relations—and their replacement by some brand new alternative set of relations. The real movement to abolish the present state of things is one of **determinate negation**, not a matter of doing away with the world as it currently exists and building a new one from scratch, but rather of subverting the current organisation of things such that a democratic and communistic organisation of production and reproduction is possible. We want to hijack and take over these processes, rather than invent new forms of organisation from the ground up in every case. Within this outlook, organisational activity becomes not a question of learning an entirely new set of skills and aptitudes but rather a matter of expanding our political world such that those with existing skills and aptitudes become committed to the possibility of applying and developing them within communist modes of organisation instead of capitalist ones. It is in this sense that *thinking as an organisation* demands not only a deep understanding of our own organisation, but also a deeper understanding of how it interacts

Albert Robida, *Phone Wooing*, from *Le Vingtième Siècle*

with, renders intelligible, and in some cases might meaningfully influence the composition and organisation of the world outside of itself. At their very best, **organisations organise**. This is how we can define the political *function* of our organisations: to organise the world differently in their social and material contexts, not as something apart from them, but rather as something that exists and builds its power by creating a political context within them.

Organisations have far greater political potential than any single individual and open up many possibilities for material and social transformation that individuals cannot. They equally do not think or act as individuals do, and many cases of friction between the individual and organisation arise from this discrepancy. It is easy to become frustrated by the fact that our organisations at times feel to be out of sync, that others in our political group are not on the same frequency as ourselves. Sometimes these frustrations themselves turn into toxic political cultures, and often they arise from a basic misunderstanding about the fact that what it means to think and act as an organisation is not at all the same thing as what it means to think and act as an individual. Synchronisation in the organisational context is something that demands work. The political strategy and agency of an organisation decomposes into processes of political discussion and democratic decision-making. We can evaluate how well these processes work and where they might be failing, but not in a way that is measured against the yardstick of individual experience. Organisations will likely act slower than an individual can react to things, but they can also act more effectively. Their possibilities for becoming quicker and more effective is not a matter of bringing their dynamics and function into line with something closer to our personal capacity for thinking and action. It demands an understanding specific to the form of organisation itself. The possibility of robust, complex, and powerful political organisations adequate to instigate revolutionary transformations of an equally complex capitalist world depends largely upon whether we can grasp this way of thinking and acting as something foundational to what the organisation is. Until we find ways of doing so, we will remain constrained by the limitations of individual subjects, of which the organisation will count as merely a glorified extension.

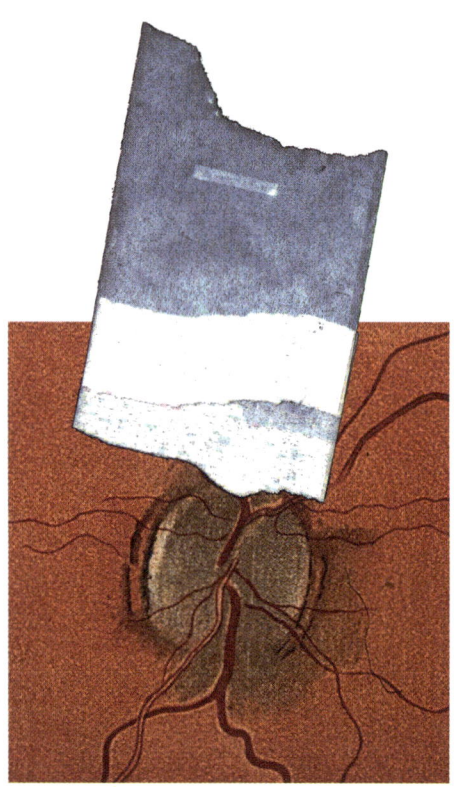

3. The Transnational Dimensions of Organisation

We have spoken about the need to think as organisations and not individuals, and so therefore to see the world around us in similar terms. We have discussed this in terms of: first, the relation of the individual to the organisation; second, the relation of the organisation to its political ecology; and third, the relation of the organisation and/or political ecology to the world as it is composed of various kinds of organisational elements. Within this, we encountered a number of ideas around how we should treat the question and limitations of the individual within the political organisation; we spoke a little about how the political organisation might strategise around both its understanding of its political ecology and its social world; we spoke about the need for higher-resolution practical knowledge of *how* both our organisations and the parts of the world they engage with function, and how this interactive process can be used to better reproduce both the organisation itself and its political practice.

In the opening section, I sought to discuss some consequences of STP's claims about organisation with respect to the idea of interpersonal ethics and culture within political organisations. These observations have been informed by my own experience and some of the frustrations that abound from it, frustrations with my own actions as much as with the actions of others. A critique of the pathologies of egoism within the space of political organisations and its effects upon the ability of that organisation to reproduce itself is not new, but we must also connect this idea to the *epistemic arrogance* that often comes with these syndromes of toxic organisational culture. By epistemic arrogance here I mean that an individual takes themselves to have the most adequate grasp of what is being addressed politically by the organisation, of the real conditions that it operates in, of what is important, of what strategic orientation it ought to have. Many of our internal debates about these questions within political organisations reflect a discursive structure that tries to answer the strategic question by asking 'well, who has the best theory?' Such a line of questioning is somehow insensitive to the context of functional political organisation and often leads to a degeneration of the necessary deliberation processes into something more like a school debating club than a serious revolutionary outfit.

The basic claim that organisations see, think, and act differently to individuals is therefore operative at the level of political strategy and practice itself, and not merely in a sense that this makes organisations nicer to be a part of, less harsh of an environment, even if those things are important in some sense too. There is a tendency to overvalue the devotion of individuals who martyr themselves to the cause, that they are somehow

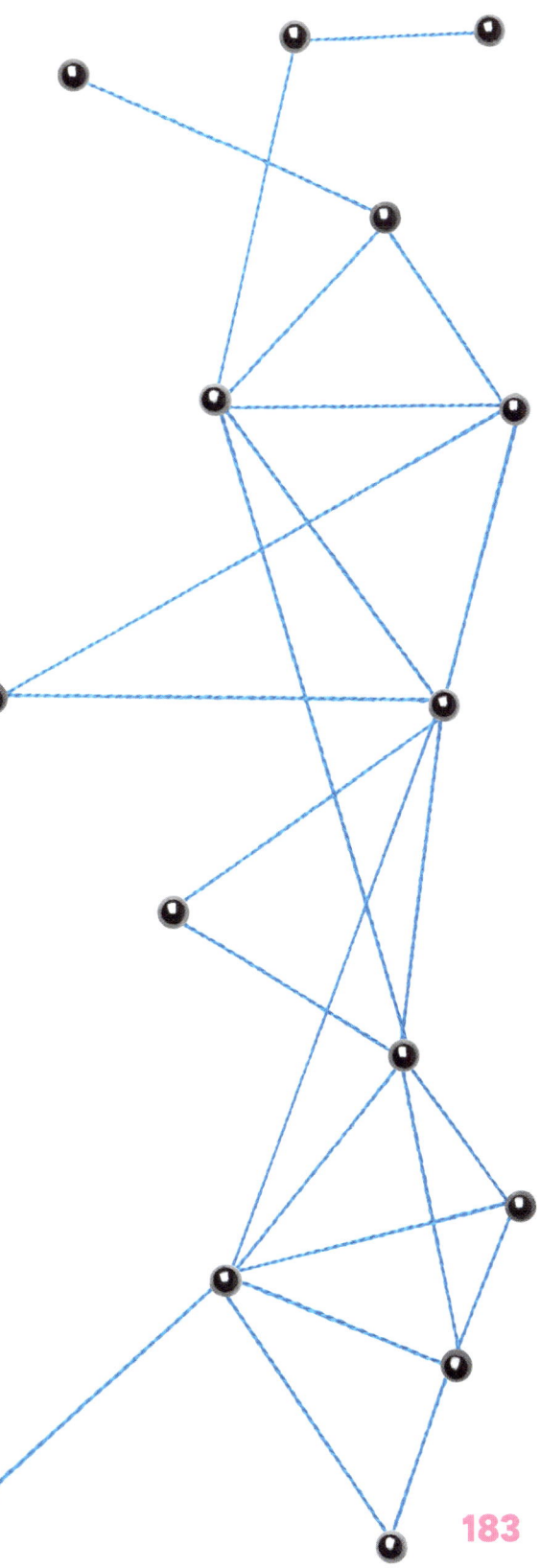

in possession of incontestable perspicacity, people whose very degree of commitment puts them on a level above other individuals and thereby of the organisation itself. The complete entanglement of their lives and politics gives them a preferential position in the decision making processes of the organisation. The precise danger of this entanglement at its limit point is, as once mentioned, that the organisation becomes an appendage of the individual, rather than the individual an appendage of the organisation. Neither of these cases is without its own dangers, and we have previously touched upon the individual's disappearance in the collective as a real threat. At the same time however, we should note that many of the dangers surrounding this latter case tend to arise under conditions where there is a mismatch between the precise ways in which individuals identify themselves with the organisation. Where some individuals' identification in the organisation reflects a contribution to a collective whole which is greater than its parts, others come to identify the whole as a mirror reflection of their own conscious agency (even if unwittingly). There are many things we could say about the subtle distinction between these two attitudes, but perhaps the most important one is that whichever of these senses of identification with the organisation predominates for any given individual has to do with the issue of *trust*. Do I trust the wisdom of my organisation as a whole, even when it falls outside the ken of my personal experience? Can I trust that the actions of my comrades are well-informed and meaningful even if I do not myself agree with their approach or tactics in every minute detail? Do I have faith in what the organisation

does and how it reproduces itself even when I am not able to supervise every action or every process that takes place? The real challenge here is that these questions may be answered in the negative either because a person has over-identified the organisation with their own egoistic self *or* because the process and structure of the organisation has not been adequately developed to ensure that these are reasonable expectations. It is in this sense that the question of organisation and the ethics of the individual within it are intimately entwined.

At the same time, we can never decisively *prove* that our structures and form of organisation are robust enough to give these assurances. Often the problem arises or is exacerbated because there is a knowledge gap between what we would need to know to have absolute confidence in the organisation (without giving in to the urge to supervise and intervene in all of its parts) and the realities of what we *can* possibly know. There is no decisive answer to this question that can be given theoretically, and like most questions concerning ethics, it can only be resolved through practice. All we can say here is that the meanings of words like *faith* and *trust* are operationally defined precisely in the context of this practical question. That is, the question of how we ought to think and act when we *don't* have enough information, and therefore must relinquish a certain sense of control over what can happen or take place. The history of authoritarian pathologies and their consequences is legible through the prism of such information problems: we could say that there is a not entirely accidental correlation between Stalin's infamous degeneration into paranoia and the degeneration of a Soviet economy and society due to the lack of reliable information signalling and management required to effectively coordinate a planned economy. Where information is lacking, overcorrections tend to ensue, and overcorrections invariably multiply themselves once a cycle of overcorrection has started. Insofar as information is always imperfect, a degree of faith in the reliability of organisation is required. But this faith is not an absolute faith, a leap of faith, the likes of which tend to characterise the existential plunging into religious belief from the lower depths of despair. The faith required is rather a question of confidence in the organisational forms we are building, their purposiveness, and the relations of comradeship they engender. In some sense also their fault tolerance, their ability to fail locally, break down in places, decompose without collapsing entirely.

It may seem somewhat strange to begin this closing section on the **transnational dimension of struggle** with such remarks. However, it is precisely in the context of transnational organisation that the affordances for control and supervision by individuals tend to most abruptly dissolve. It is not that transnational organisation is the only context in which we must begin to think as organisations, but rather that the very possibility of genuinely transnational organisation depends on cultivating this kind of relation. A particular pitfall of transnational organisation is that the meetings and structures we develop might ultimately become extraterritorial zones of exception, a cosmopolitan meeting space which develops its own organisational habits and language amongst those who participate and which remains ultimately disconnected to larger struggles in those regions being represented and the larger social bases in their territories. The task of transnational organising is to create an organisational continuum between disparate territories, to create shared political contexts where we are currently only capable of pointing to the fact *that* compositions of capital present in one territory are linked to flows that traverse and appear in others, but not precisely *how* they do. This demands a degree of organisation and coordination, even synchronicity, between disparate political forces at disparate locations in ways that make it practically *impossible* to supervise what one's comrades are doing. Interestingly, we can observe here that the possibility of a genuine transnational platform requires that organisations can act together in a manner of coordination which precisely does *not* recommend that they become subsumed within a single organisational structure. It demands instead that we find ways to build affinities and assemble transient forms of organisational unity that are built upon the work of creating and maintaining compatibility between organisations and movements which are decidedly *distinct* entities, and remain so through the process of coordinated activity. In this context, we simply cannot afford to suffer the neuroses of individuals who over-identify with the organisation itself, who continue to insist that the only form in which strategic and political questions can be rendered is in that which appears naturally to the form of individual consciousness.

Aside from the question of how we organise ourselves, there is also an important lesson about how capital is composed and organises itself which arises in the context of struggle at the transnational level. The reality of capital's composition in most instances inevitably points to a dimension that transcends the local and demands a transnational view. This is another way of pointing to the fact that any basic structure of capital we may try to address invariably includes a transnational dimension, that it cannot be described in a politically meaningful way without reference to its transnational character. From the standpoint of revolutionary left politics, there is no coherent way of addressing commodity production in the modern era without taking full account of *transnational* value chains, from sites of extraction, to outsourcing of manufacturing labour, to legal jurisdictions, to logistics networks.

DELETE, *Untitled*

Once again, it is not sufficient to know *that* all such elements in a production chain may take place in different locations, we must understand *how* these chains function effectively, precisely because they are organised in this way. One significant challenge of transnational organising is to find forms of political practice adequate to uncovering the organisational composition of capital not merely through research of information available within the public domain, but through forms of political activity which 'sense' the realities of capital within different fields of struggle and are thereby capable of articulating a practical politics opposing them. This can take a number of possible forms, and it would be mistaken to try to articulate or uncover which particular form of intervention is the best. The multifaceted reality of capitalism and its transnational character recommends that we must employ a diversity of strategies that incorporate site-specific, context-sensitive interventions that are grounded in a sequence of organisational learning and methodological development, as well as being sensitive to the organisational form through which they are carried out. It doesn't make sense to attempt a strike with a very small close-knit group of actionists, but we should not conclude from this basic fact that the strike is the only adequate tactic for political struggle or that the only useful form of political organisation is one which incorporates a large base, as trade unions often do. The question of organisation at the level of political ecologies is one of asking how these different forms of organisation can be made compatible, if not even synchronised in certain cases at the tactical level. A closely-related but distinct question is how organisation in different territories, by different groups with their own organisational history, methodologies, and context-sensitive operational knowledge can be brought into some kind of transnational convergence. The precise question of *how* such groups can be linked, of *building* a shared political context depends largely upon the possibility of engaging in organisational enquiry between such disparate groups. At this point, the practical methodologies of the Common Space of Organisations (CSO) become an incredibly useful tool. [13]

13. A summary presentation with some visual representation of how CSO works and its relationship to STP can be found here: https://www.youtube.com/watch?v=P7uEhKeeQRA&ab_channel=SubsetofTheoreticalPractice

Albert Robida, *The Revolution of 195*, from *Le Vingtième Siècle*

As stated in the outset of the previous paragraph, the challenge we face at the transnational level is not simply to research the transnational dimensions of capital through what is available to us in the public domain, but rather to find some way of creating a shared context of political struggle through the harnessing of practically-oriented knowledge available to us only once we materially interact with and investigate the organisational composition of capital. At the transnational level, it becomes all the more apparent that a shared sense of political identity or symbolic allegiances is not enough or the important thing that connects us. What is needed is a set of shared practical orientations with respect to transnational capital. This shared orientation does not benefit from any process to unify different organisations with a generic and top-down understanding of strategy, not only because such approaches impose unnecessary constraints upon organisations struggling within their particular contexts, but also because it is a completely counterproductive approach. **To build a shared political context and derive a strategic orientation from it requires a labour of organisational enquiry, a form of** activity which more directly links political struggles. **This represents nothing less than the possibility of consolidating the lessons of concrete interactions with capital on a higher dimension than what is even possible within a single organisation alone. It is not a matter of merely presenting results and findings, but connecting them within a shared context that can be operationalised in political practice and strategy.** It is the subtle but important distinction between knowing *that* parallel processes of capital reproducing itself take place in ways that are synchronised between different locations, and uncovering *how* they are synchronised. Accordingly we should develop our own forms of synchronous political activity at the transnational level adequate to addressing these problems.

One final aspect of transnational organisation that we should turn our attention to before concluding is the communisation of the transnational structures of capitalism. Throughout much of this essay, there has been a particular emphasis on understanding the composition of capital in a sense that has more to do with the possibility of its decomposition within the idiom of struggle. That is, we have spoken mainly about how to confront and oppose the structures of capitalism that oppress and alienate us. Conversely, we have addressed the need to think organisationally in a more constructive or positive sense mainly in ways that have to do with our *political organisations*. I would like, however, to now finally consider how understanding the compositional realities of transnational capital can also be important for a revolutionary horizon which is not merely

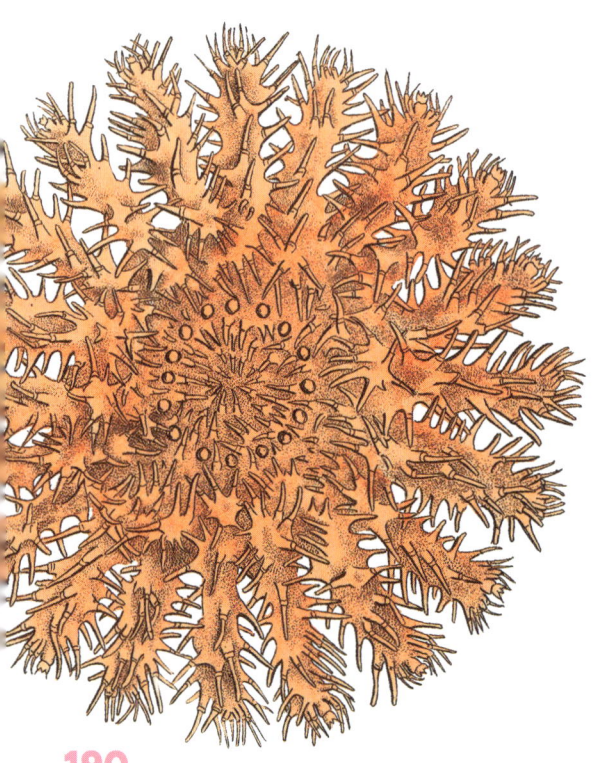

destructive. All that is solid may well melt into air, but thin air does not congeal itself into something solid, so we need to think about what a revolution would mean as the negation of what we have rather than the ideal wish for what we have not.

Here, we can draw upon the idea of **communisation**, whose history and development has been helpfully articulated by Endnotes[14], to proffer an alternative understanding of the usefulness of decomposing capital at a transnational level. I have already mentioned the example of how effective strike action can lay bare the realities of how capital is composed organisationally. However, the decomposition of the structures of transnational capital is not done with a view to completely abolishing them, and strike activity should not be viewed as an imminent critique to the forms of social production that are being disrupted and decomposed in their entirety. This point becomes obvious once we consider the fact that the moment of strike is a transient event. It is not sustainable as a more persistent state of society. The breaking down of some composition of capital does not by itself promise a better world let alone a solution to the political problems it poses. It is also not advisable to retreat into a comforting theory about how the very event of breakdown automatically yields to the recovery of humankind's 'unspoiled pre-capitalist nature.' The purpose of any strike is not to prove that human beings are ultimately capable of living independently without the forms of production that come apart when labour is suddenly withdrawn, but rather expresses exactly the inverse. The latent paradox here in the notion of a deeply political strike is that at a more local strategic level it may advocate the need for a return to labour and production on better terms for the workers,

---

14. Endnotes. Communisation and Value-Form Theory by Endnotes. https://endnotes.org.uk/articles/4. Accessed 4 Mar. 2025.

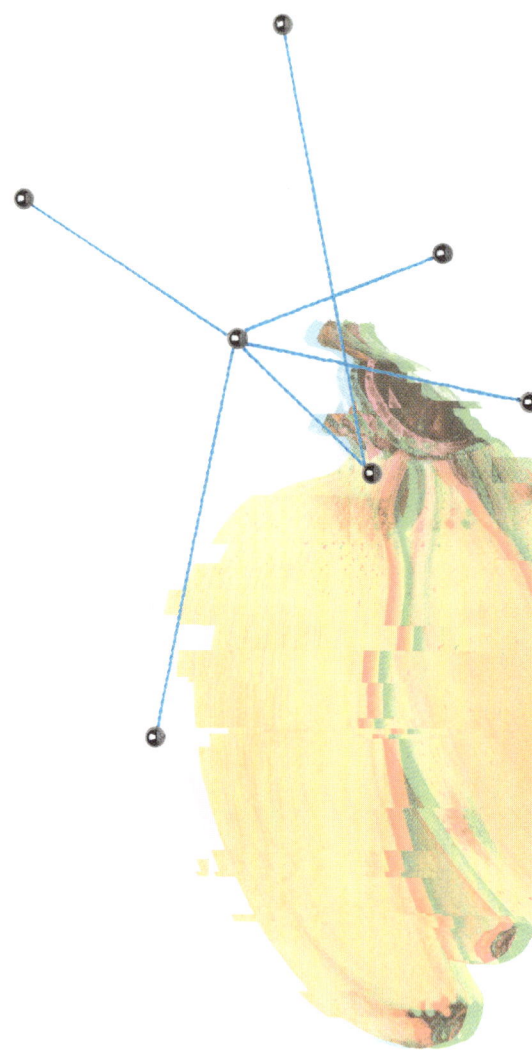

the transnational scale where this precise point is least understood, not least since a very crude critique of 'globalisation' tends to understand the dependency relations instantiated by transnational forms of production as some kind of pathology or syndrome that can be resolved by an absolute return to the local. In other words, that no social or material need satisfied by transnational capital is a *real and genuine* need.

What do these transient moments of decomposition actually tell us then? The answer to this question comes neither in the form 'Ah, now we've realised that transnational logistics networks are completely unnecessary, and we must struggle to abolish them everywhere', *nor* 'Ah, now we that we understand how dependent our everyday life is upon the transnational value chain, we must only limit ourselves to positional struggle and better conditions for workers, since the world is far too complex and would collapse if we tried to displace these chains or any part of them'. The strike action itself, or any other form of disruptive intervention for that matter, does not immediately show us that we are dependent in every sense or that we are independent in every sense from capitalist relations of production. On the other hand, these actions can furnish a number of politically actionable revelations. Firstly, decomposing the concrete operations of capital allows us to think about what parts in a value chain can be displaced, where precisely militant struggle may be necessary in order to heighten social contradictions, and how this activity itself may be integrated with other forms of synchronous political activity which support it. For instance, we may acknowledge a contemporary social and material dependency on certain

whilst on a more general political level it articulates the need for a revolutionary re-organisation of the very form and relations of production themselves. Holding onto the latter of these makes it possible for us to consider the decompositional act of the strike as something more than a tactical manoeuvre within an attritional struggle for position within the capitalist system. Just as this is true of strikes at the local and national level, so is it at the level of the transnational: it is often at imported foods—say, bananas— that cannot be grown or cultivated in an efficient way in many territories that consume them. It may even be possible for people in such territories to live or learn to live without bananas as an essential part of their diet, but may also be a completely counterproductive revolutionary strategy to argue the case for this and militantly agitate for a complete halt to the production chain for this good.

It may, on the other hand, be necessary to organise a transnational strike at multiple sites of production and logistics to make this dependency practically apparent on the social level. The point of doing so is *not* to say that people can and should live without access to bananas. It is not to claim that because this dependency is socially and historically constructed, we therefore must learn to live without this need. No such project would improve the lives of agricultural workers in the decolonial countries where bananas are cultivated en masse, and in many ways may worsen their situation in the short run. The entire point of bringing into relief this compositional network of production and distribution by temporarily bringing it to a halt is to illuminate the precise forms of exploitation that do take place within it and understand exactly *how* they allow this structure of capitalist production to sustain itself. Consequently, in the material organisation of alternative social arrangements, the task is not to learn how to become materially self-sufficient with respect to nutrition at the level of national economies.

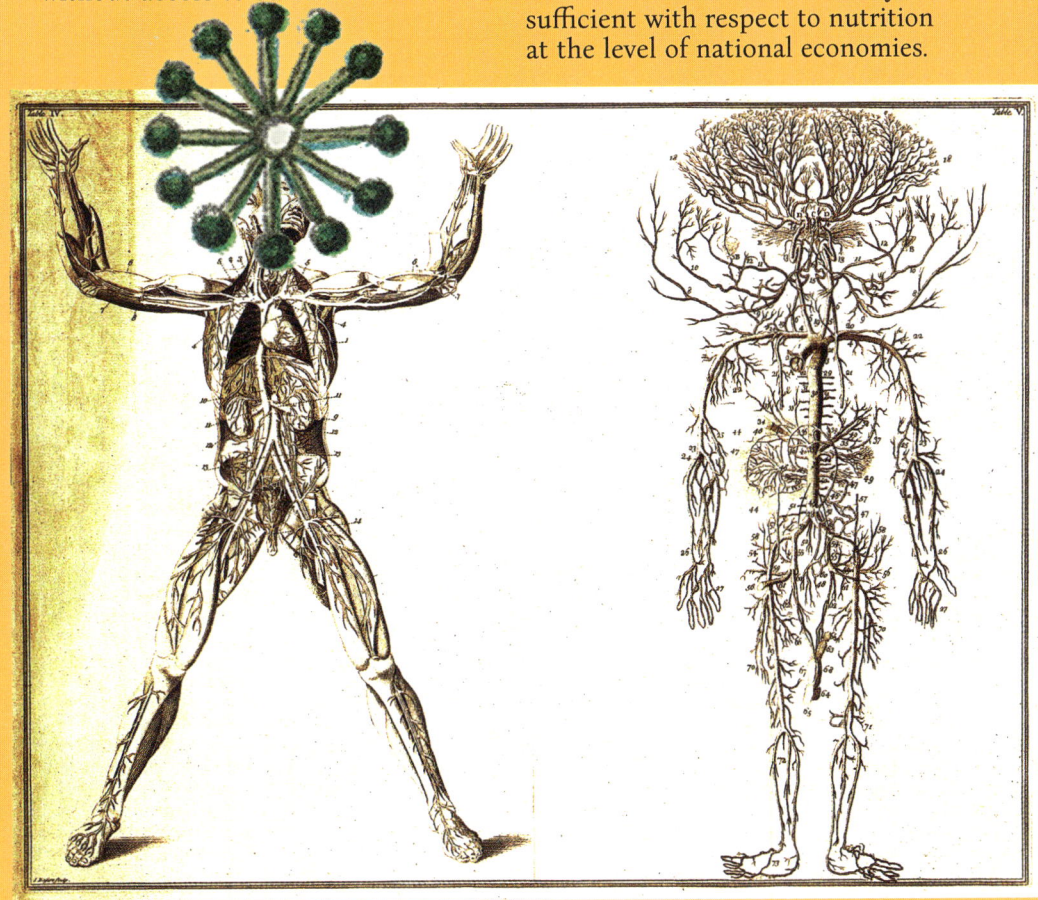

John Augustus Knapp, A Metal Boat

Instead, it is to work through in some practical and organisational sense how it might be possible to satisfy a need, both without trying to convince people of the necessity of eliminating this need, and also without accepting the forms of exploitation that make the satisfaction of this need possible under existing social arrangements made possible by severe global inequality. This does not mean that all socially-constructed needs are valid, and that all must be accommodated no matter the cost. It does not mean that we should enter into a calculation of lessening the exploitation of workers in the global south to whatever degree possible whilst maintaining the level of production required to satisfy consumption demands elsewhere. Rather, the point is to engender a situation where it is possible to negotiate the accommodation of social needs without exploitation taking place. To understand to what extent they are capable of being accommodated in a fair and just way.

To reconfigure the social dimension of need by eliminating the aspect of it dependent upon exploitation without eliminating the need entirely, to whatever extent this is possible. Insofar as the strike opens up and illuminates the composition of capitalist arrangements that satisfy the existing demand for a commodity in one place, it also gives us some kind of practical orientation about the question of how and to what extent those social needs could still be accommodated under communistic social arrangements. It asks what precise parts of that organisational structure would need to be reconfigured, and how do we go about doing it.

The question of need here is also variably expressed and itself called into question by the kind of disruptive decompositional process just described. It may certainly be the case that we realise that some needs are simply not worth accommodating

194

politically because any possible organisation of production around the satisfaction of these needs demands an intolerable degree of exploitation somewhere along the production chain. In other words, it is practically not possible to replace a transnational capitalist structure with a communist one, and so our strategic focus does need to be that of making it more difficult for that capitalist structure to exist. The case of fossil fuels is undeniably such an example. But even here, the revolutionary strategy for a complete weening of all social needs from fossil fuel dependency should not involve a moralising elimination of those needs. Concerted attempts to work out how such needs can be accommodated through renewable energy sources are needed, and it makes perfect sense to draw upon the resources of transnational coordination to do this. Just as non-renewable energy sources are found in abundance in some territories and not in others, and therefore require transnational networks of production, we should not rule out the possibility that transnational affordances can also be harnessed in the case of renewable energy production.

The basic conviction of this thesis here is that it is ultimately possible on some level to replace many such capitalist structures with communist ones, and indeed that it is possible to imagine a revolutionary horizon in which it is harder for capitalist structures to exist than it is for communist ones, an exact inversion of the present state of things. Need itself is a category which should be thought of as sensitive to this kind of interplay surrounding production and reproduction. The expression of a need implies that we should work politically towards its fulfilment but not that it should be immediately satisfied by any means and at all costs. Of course, we understand the social construction of need under capitalist society as invariably created by the commodity form. The argument here, from a strategic perspective, is simply that we cannot go about abolishing these needs in a sense that denies some reality to their social construction. We must try to imagine a transition towards communist society by seeking to fulfil forms of social and material dependency through a communist mode of production. We must work out the practicalities of such production by attempting to satisfy well-defined

social needs to whatever extent we can, and this likely includes needs that can only be accommodated through social production on a transnational scale. This goes even more so for the question of how we can accommodate and satisfy the very acute material needs of many post-colonial societies, given that more often than not such needs are not in any case being satisfied by the capitalist mode of production.

The practicalities surrounding these questions can never be sufficiently addressed in a single essay such as this one, let alone in the written form of a theoretical argument. My contention concerning the need to think organisationally, and the specific form its elaboration has taken in the above, are not concerns of theoretical production for its own sake however. Rather, they arise entirely from a context of political practice, both in the sense of how we navigate and struggle within our own organisations, and how we strive to struggle as organisations within the wider context of the world. I've offered little by way of precise recommendations, and many of the examples I have tried to provide will no doubt also prove faulty in one way or another. This much is intended. It has already been mentioned that we often look to political theory and reflection for a kind of silver bullet, a form of revelation which will allow us to decisively break the deadlock we inevitably encounter in our own political practice. This understanding is deeply misguided, above all because it isolates the moment of theoretical reflection as something separate from political activity and which can be considered as completed once we have found the particular insight we were looking for. But political insights do not come in the form of a single revelation that changes everything. Theoretical activity, just as much as material political struggle, is an arduous and often unyielding form of practice. We must remain consistent in our engagement. It is a lifelong conquest, there is no point in time at which we can say we have finally understood, no point in the struggle where we will finally be free of all forms of oppression and exploitation. The most we can hope for is a moment when it suddenly begins to feel as though the tide has turned, a point where we suddenly realise that what was unthinkable at some earlier point in our lives is now a reality. Perhaps one signal merit of thinking organisationally is that however dissatisfying our outlook may be at the level of personal experience, the organisation itself endures at a scale far exceeding that of the individual. Politically-speaking, it makes more sense to work on our organisations than it does to work on ourselves.

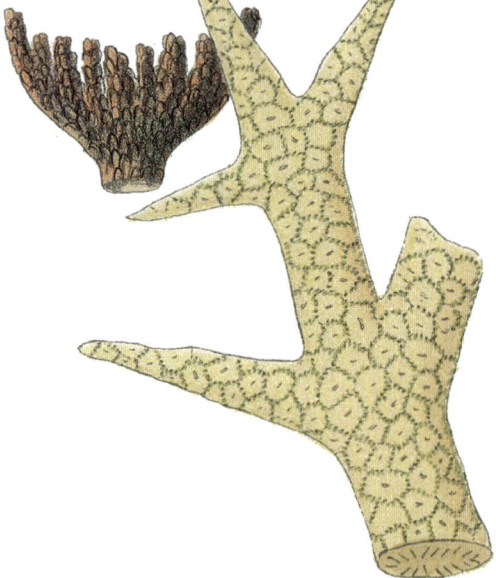

Théophile-Alexandre Steinlen, *Communards' Wall* from *Le Chambourd Socialiste*

Theo F.

BENEATH THE TOMBSTONES, THE BEACH

an interview with John G., aka TheLitCritGuy

Odilon Redon, *Hideous Larvae*

TF: As an introduction for those unfamiliar with you, could you explain yourself, your blog, and your work as a podcaster on Horror Vanguard?

JG: I am an author and writer who has been publishing work on culture, theory and film for about a decade now. In that time, I've worked my way through a PhD, and published four books on horror, religion and politics before leaving academia. My research was originally on nineteenth century Gothic literature, seeing in it a series of theological and religious metaphors that responded to social and political fears of the time. Midway through my PhD I watched a talk by China Miéville, on Marxism and Halloween—you can still find it on YouTube—and it essentially completely rewired my thinking on what seemed like a very antiquated mode of culture and brought it home to me in all of its immediacy. This was my introduction to a lot of contemporary horror films and also a lot of contemporary theory. It was around this time that I found some of Mark Fisher's work, and like many of us who came up in the post-2008 moment, it was another profoundly formative encounter.

From there, me and my friend started Horror Vanguard as a space for us to try and talk through ideas, bringing together horror films, theory and philosophy. It's become something far larger and stranger than we predicted, and I think we've opened up space for the bringing together of contemporary horror culture with the wider horrors of contemporary capitalism.

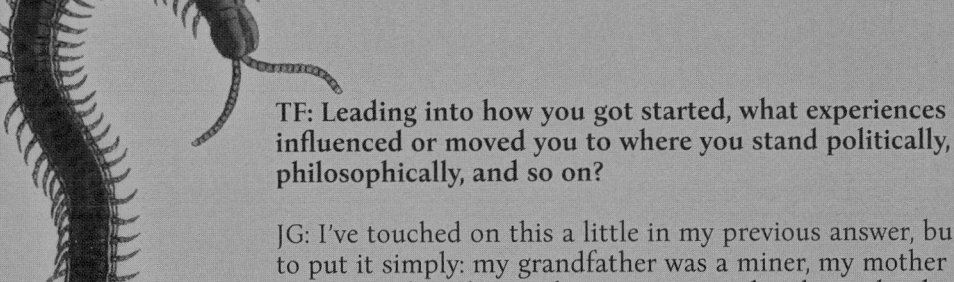

TF: **Leading into how you got started, what experiences influenced or moved you to where you stand politically, philosophically, and so on?**

JG: I've touched on this a little in my previous answer, but to put it simply: my grandfather was a miner, my mother was a social worker, and I grew up in a deindustrialised town in the north of England. Then, I graduated university in 2008 when the global capitalist system went through a serious crisis. From there, in the UK, came a generation of austerity in which neoliberal consensus was enforced by wealthy politicians and so many of the mechanisms by which one could make a life were taken away. Things like a university education that didn't immiserate you with debt, rent low enough to spend some time being creative or writing or making art, jobs that provided enough in wages or even mundane things like a social safety net that would mean a mother with children might be able to feed her family every week. The last fifteen years or so in the UK felt in many ways like a vicious contraction—a horizon collapsing in on us. What is most essential is the intellectual effort to look beyond that horizon for something better—this is the rupture known as Utopia.

Harry Clarke, *Detestable Putridity*

Odilon Redon, *The Chimera Gazed at All Things With Fear*

TF: Earlier this year, you released *A Primer on Utopian Philosophy: An Introduction to the Work of Ernst Bloch* as part of the 'Zero Utopia' series. For those unfamiliar, can you explain Bloch's relationship to the struggles in the last century towards Utopia and his conceptions of Hope, the Not-Yet and Non-Synchronicity?

JG: This is a long and complex topic—to which the Primer was supposed to be a short answer. Bloch is a fascinating and very dense philosopher, who influenced a whole generation of Marxists and communists: Lukács, Adorno and Benjamin were all writing in response to and in the aftermath of Bloch. He was a brilliant polymath philosopher and his colossal three volume work *The Principle of Hope* is a high point of twentieth century philosophy. For Bloch, hope is not simply a fleeting momentary emotion, or a high point of political agency.

Rather, for Bloch, hope is a philosophical impulse, one which is orientated towards the future. Hope is about a qualitative and quantitative rupture with the way things are—and to try and make this claim, Bloch essentially has to try and reconstruct philosophy and politics from the ground up. Fredric Jameson wrote one of the earliest English language introductions to Bloch's philosophy in his book 'Marxism and Form', and Jameson describes it as a philosophy of the future, like a satellite that has crashed to earth, covered in hieroglyphs still to be decoded. Hope is an impulse of history itself for Bloch—and so the opposite of hope for Bloch is not fear (which is too, in its way, about what might happen in the future). Rather, the opposite of hope is nostalgia or memory—looking back at what we've lost rather than pressing forward to what we have to make. It's why the concept of the Not Yet is so important—Bloch uses the term 'Ungleichzeitigket' or non-synchronicity. The Not Yet is the political articulation of an important philosophical point—namely, that capitalist history is incomplete, that the closure of the present is never total. As Bloch puts it, 'not all people live in the same Now'—the present is full of these ruptures, and moments of uneven development. This is a pretty straightforward Marxist point but in some more metaphysical and philosophical language. For an example of how history can become a part of revolutionary action, think of 'The Eighteenth Brumaire':

'The tradition of all dead generations weighs like a nightmare on the brains of the living. And just as they seem to be occupied with revolutionizing themselves and things, creating something that did not exist before, precisely in such epochs of revolutionary crisis they anxiously conjure up the spirits of the past to their service, borrowing from them names, battle slogans, and costumes in order to present this new scene in world history in time-honored disguise and borrowed language. Thus, Luther put on the mask of the Apostle Paul, the Revolution of 1789-1814 draped itself alternately in the guise of the Roman Republic and the Roman Empire, and the Revolution of 1848 knew nothing better to do than to parody, now 1789, now the revolutionary tradition of 1793-95.'

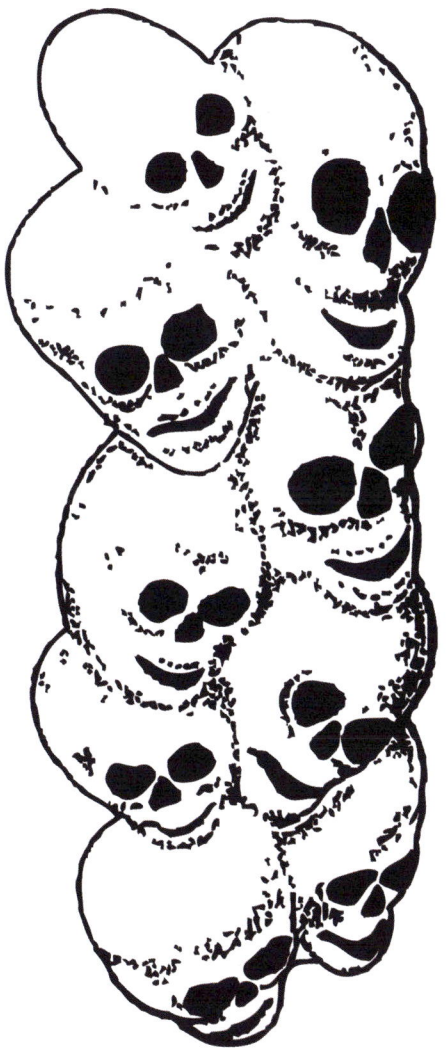

Bloch sees the process as part of the very structure of history, from the ways in which old beliefs and folklore persists to older political impulses that make themselves in the present. The Not Yet is used in a variety of ways in Blochs work—I tried to flesh out some of the ways this term can be used in the Primer:

Firstly, there is something that is not actually now but something which has a kind of actuality. The child is not yet an adult but possesses in that incompleteness a potential to become one. Yet the term isn't just future-orientated, it can be taken to mean something like 'not so far', or even something which has failed to come to fruition. The ambiguity is stronger in the original German as Bloch's 'noch-nicht' can be translated as both not yet and still not. Here then, Bloch models a kind of Janus theory: looking back to a past in order to find the conditions, potentialities and resources by which the future might come into being—not simply historically, or even politically, but ontologically and existentially. At the same time, Bloch is looking to a future, a Utopia, which is not programmatic or deterministic, but the ever-unfolding process that is an integral part of both human nature and all of existence itself.

TF: In your book, *Capitalism: A Horror Story*, the main thread running through is that Gothic Marxism, which runs on a critical un-realism, can be described as an antidote in many ways to Mark Fisher's Acid Communism. Can you elaborate on this connection? To what extent does Gothic Marxism develop class-consciousness?

JG: I would say that the two things are in many ways complementary—I think it's obvious I've been massively influenced by Mark's work. In my book I describe Gothic Marxism as something akin to the dark counterpart or shadow of Acid Communism. The unfinished introduction to what would have been a book on Acid Communism opens with the sentence that 'The claim of the book is that the last forty years have been about the exorcising of "the spectre of a world which could be free"'. Here I think Gothic Marxism is a good means for engaging with spectres—they are in the history of the Gothic almost always heralds of loss, and therefore less about our fear than they are about our grief. At the same time, the ghost is always that which has returned—we thought someone was gone, and yet here they are again. We're forced to look back at a history that we thought was settled—dead and buried—and at the same time, the return of history opens the possibility of the future. That spectre of a world that could be free is what haunts the collective cultural imagination of a world under Capitalist Realism, and yet the Gothic and horror consistently show us that everything we thought was gone is all too ready to clamber out of its shallow grave.

TF: A key split that Bloch makes in his Marxism is between that of the Cold and Warm streams, so my question to you is what is significant about this distinction? How does this project of Gothic Marxism relate to the opening of communist horizons today, the synthesis of Cold and Warm streams, and their necessity in class war today?

JG: So for Bloch there are two tendencies or modes of Marxist thinking. First, there is the Cold stream: the rigorous critique of all that exists and a focus on materialism and political economy. On the other hand is the Warm stream: the almost prophetic, future oriented language of the *Communist Manifesto*. One tends towards the quantitative, the other the qualitative. For Bloch, both of these ways of working are essential. Without a utopian future as a horizon to move towards, Marxist politics loses itself in obscurantism. However, Bloch said the Warm stream of Marxism needs 'lead pouring into its shoes' to keep it grounded and focused on the struggles

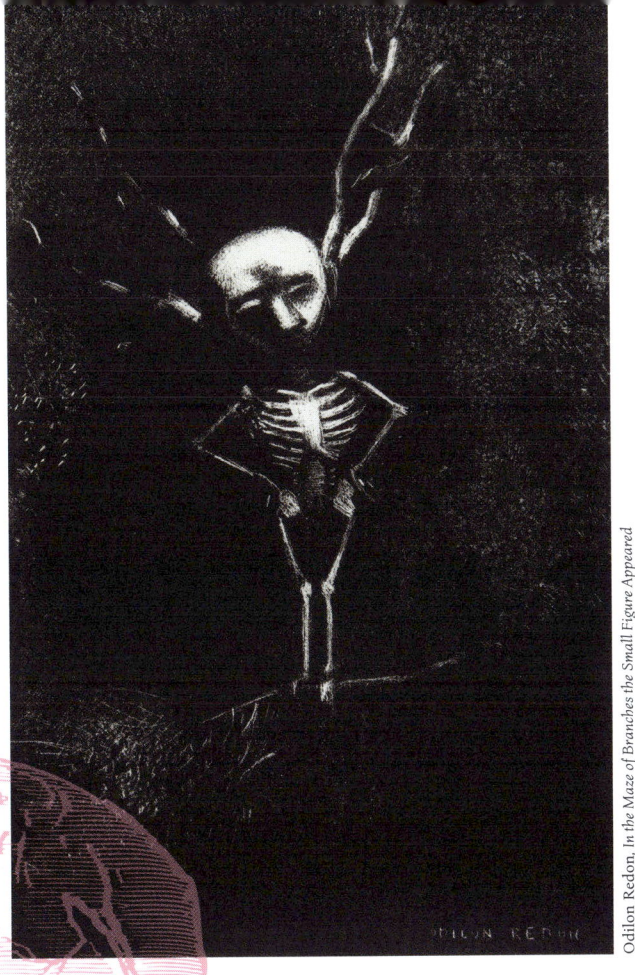

Odilon Redon, *In the Maze of Branches the Small Figure Appeared*

at hand. The significance is clear—the last thirty years or so have seen a colossal contraction of the radical imagination—this is what made the diagnosis of Mark Fisher's *Capitalist Realism* so compelling and resonant (and for all his reputation as a miserabilist, Fisher was profoundly Utopian in many ways). In the case of my work on Gothic Marxism, my book *Capitalism: A Horror Story* tries to position it within the tradition of romantic anticapitalism and as a way of imaginatively responding to the phenomenological and subjective horrors of life under capitalism. I think there is a necessity for such a response—after all, as Mark put it, emancipatory politics must always destroy the appearance of a natural order. The metaphors of horror films are metaphors, yes, but they are also real! Horror films can be a very powerful way of bringing home that reality and of underscoring that the naturalised reality of our capitalist present is, in actuality, a constructed horror story in which we need to act collectively.

TF: You generally point to horror as this way of opening up the possible realisations of the problematics facing us today as communists, be that of the Saw franchise as the epitome of the cruelty endemic to neoliberalism and the FIRE economy. What horror media would you recommend to those seeking a communist politics baked into it?

JG: I can't help but think of *Mary Shelley's Frankenstein*. If you haven't read it, or haven't read it in a while, it's a novel all about the emergence of a particular kind of subjectivity, which is at the same time, a collective. Remember, the creature that is brought to life is stitched together from the bodies of the poor and the destitute into something so powerful, eloquent and—in a way—revolutionary. There is a quote from the novel, spoken by the creature that I really like: 'Life, although it may only be an accumulation of anguish, is dear to me, and I will defend it.' Horror is in no short supply but life is still dear, and worth defending.

TF: To round this interview out, what projects are you working on at the moment and what struggles make you hopeful for the programmatic 'reform of consciousness' as Marx put it?

JG: Currently I'm working on a sequel or follow-up of sorts to *Capitalism: A Horror Story* focusing on the relationships between subjectivity, housing, debt, mortgages and haunted houses. Post-2008 we've seen a huge resurgence in the haunted house film, and at times of economic instability we all become painfully aware of the fragility and contingency of our homes.

In terms of struggles, the direct action towards weapons manufacturing by Palestine Action is a burning testimony to the vital importance of the fact that horrors in which we are entangled demand action. The wider environmental struggle of direct action and (as argued by Andreas Malm, the destruction of private property) is again a reflection of the line from Frankenstein, that in all the anguish of our shared world, life is worth defending. 🌸

Edouard de Beaumont, *Ghosts of His Own Making*

Théophile-Alexandre Steinlen, from *Le Chambourd Socialiste*

A Note Regarding Images

This publication could not have looked the way it does without the many works which make up the digital commons. I am immensely grateful to all those who contribute to the communal riches that surround us, including those who work to make sure that public domain images are easily accessible and usable in transformative art and design work.

I am paricularly grateful to the Old Book Illustrations project (oldbookillustrations.com), the Heritage Library (heritagetype.com), Resource Boy (resourceboy.com), and to the photographers of unsplash.com. Thanks also to DELETE for the use of their artwork.

I have tried to credit images, whether public domain or not. While not strictly necessary in most cases, it felt like a good practice in an age where we're often caught between an oppressive system of commercialised copyrights on one hand, and the exploitation and theft of artists' labour on the other. Some of the titles are somewhat loose as many of the works were originally intended to illustrate other texts; in these cases I used titles only to facilitate finding the images in existing databases, although a couple of times I've also mentioned the text name for added context (for example, the delightful *Le Vingtième Siècle* published in 1883, which is full of illustrations of an imagined 20th century)

If public domain images are uncredited, it's because they had already been modified, remixed and repackaged such that I couldn't find the original artist. Any uncredited images not in the public domain were sourced from image repositories such as rawpixel under either CC0 or a standard business licence, and did not come with an artist's name attached. Named or not, I am thankful for and appreciative of their work.

Flann D.

DELETE, *Untitled*